Foreword by Adam Wainwright – pitcher for the St. Louis Cardinals

LIFE IN THE FAIRWAY

what golf teaches us about integrity

CHAD BONHAM

Featuring stories & commentary
from PGA Golfers

Cink Byrd Simpson Crane

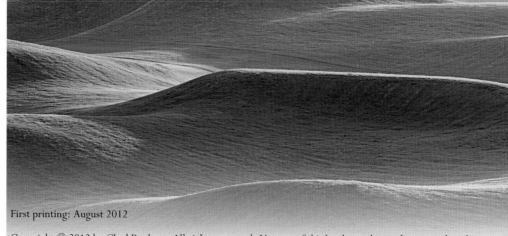

First printing: August 2012

New Leaf Press, P.O. Box 726, Green Forest, AR 72638
New Leaf Press is a division of the New Leaf Publishing Group, Inc.

ISBN: 978-0-89221-714-4
Library of Congress Number: 2012937813

Cover by Justin Skinner & Diana Bogardus
Interior Design by Diana Bogardus

Unless otherwise noted, Scripture quotations are from the New International Version of the Bible.

Please consider requesting that a copy of this volume be purchased by your local library system.

Printed in China

Please visit our website for other great titles: www.newleafpress.net

For information regarding author interviews, please contact the publicity department at (870) 438-5288

Photo Credits: T-top, B-bottom, L-left, R-right

Lindy Thompson Golden Isles Photography: pg 6-7, pg 21, pg 24-25, pg 27

Jonathan & Amanda Byrd: pg 19, pg 20 (2), pg 22T, pg 23 (3)

Webb & Dowd Simpson: pg 34, pg 35, pg 36B (2), pg 40 (2), pg 41, pg 45

Chad Bonham: pg 55, pg 71, pg 75

Stewart Cink: pg 54 (3), pg 58L, pg 59

Ben & Heather Crane and Doug Crane: pg 69 (2), pg 70, pg 72B (3), pg 73T (2), pg 75

Kevin & Courtney Streelman: pg 85, pg 86 (4), pg 87

D.J. Brigman: pg 89 (2), pg 90 (3), pg 91

Bernhard Langer: pg 93 (2), pg 94 (2), pg 95

Bill Satterfield (www.GolfCourseGurus.com) pg 77, pg 88, pg 92

Diana Bogardus: pg 8-9, pg 17

Tim Dudley: pg 26, pg65

Shutterstock.com: pg 2-3, pg 4, pg 5, pg 11, pg 15 (3), pg 16, pg 29, pg 33, pg 36 T, pg 37, pg 38 (2), pg 39, pg 42 (2), pg 43, pg 47, pg 48-49T, pg 48 b (2), pg 50-51, pg 52, pg 57, pg 58R, pg 61, pg 63, pg 64, pg 65T, pg 67, pg 68, pg 72T, pg 73B, pg 74, pg 76, pg 78, pg 79, pg 80, pg 81, pg 82 (2), pg 83, pg 84, pg 97, pg 100, pg 101, pg 102 (3), pg 103, pg 104, pg 105 (2), pg 106 (2), pg 106-107, pg 109, pg 112

istock.com: pg 12TL, pg 22, pg 60, pg 89B,

Flickr Commons: pg. 12B, pg 14T, pg 30 (2), pg 31 (2)

wikipedia: pg 44, pg 84

Library of Congress: pg 13, pg 14B

New Leaf Press
A Division of New Leaf Publishing Group
www.newleafpress.net

Every time I am blessed with the opportunity to write my acknowledgments, I can't help but be blown away by how gracious the Lord has been to first bless me with a small measure of talent and ability and then in allowing me to use it to produce published materials that will hopefully make an impact on someone's life.

Of course, my first earthly thanks go to my wife, Amy, and my incredible boys Lance, Cole, and Quinn. I am nothing without them, and my purpose in life is to first and foremost glorify God through my role as a husband and father. I've learned a lot about myself while writing this book that I know has challenged me to a higher level of integrity.

My mother, Betty Bonham, is an angel, a saint, and a warrior all rolled up into one amazing human being. She's a huge reason behind why I do what I do. She and my father, Stan (who is currently having a pretty sweet time in heaven), provided me a spiritual, emotional, and creative foundation upon which I safely stand. And I always have to thank my sister Rhonda Dilldine and her husband, Dusty, and their daughters, Elizabeth and Madison, as well as my sister Karla Partridge and her husband, Denton, for the years of unconditional love and unfettered support.

Thanks to Tim Dudley who allowed me to sit with him and his team back in November of 2010 and talk about an array of ideas. When he said the words, "You know, there hasn't been a good golf book out there in while," who knew it would result in this incredibly satisfying project. I also want to thank Laura Welch, Craig Froman, and the rest of the New Leaf Publishing editorial, design, and marketing team for getting behind the book, making it better, and pushing it to the biggest audience possible.

It's quite obvious that this book is only worth reading largely due to the contributions and support of the athletes who so generously lent their insights and their name recognition: Jonathan Byrd, Stewart Cink, Ben Crane, Webb Simpson, Adam Wainwright, Aaron Baddeley, D.J. Brigman, Bernhard Langer, Justin Leonard, and Kevin Streelman. It was an honor to tell your stories and to get to know you a little better in the process.

Other special thanks go to these fine folks and groups that contributed or helped in one way or another: Morris Pickens, Golden Isles FCA, Rand Jerris, Michael Trostel, Thomas Pagel, Lew Blakely, USGA Museum, Gary Wiren, Heather Crane, Doug Crane, Dowd Simpson, Ron Baddeley, Ben Bost, Tour Life, FCA Golf, Larry Moody, Brad Payne, Nick Doster, Eva Stiller, David Hinkle, Hambric Sports, Courtney Streelman, Tom Lehman, Mark Wilson, Rickie Fowler, Tony Guadagnolo, Lindy Thompson, Rob and Anne Cink, Golden Isles Photography, Michelle Allan, and Crown Sports Management.

My prayer is that you will all be pleased with the end result and encouraged to know that, thanks to this collaborative effort, many who skim these pages will be challenged to pursue a greater level of Christ-centered integrity in their lives.

— Chad Bonham

"Integrity is doing what's right even though no one is around. You might be all alone at home, in a hotel, or wherever. It's the choices you make then that determine whether or not you're going to live a life of integrity. When I travel without the family, it's the choices I make of what to watch on TV, what to read and what my eyes see. It's when I'm on the golf course and the ball moves and no one sees it except for me and I call the penalty on myself. It's not just a single choice, but it's one choice after another that leads to a life of integrity."

— Aaron Baddeley

TABLE OF CONTENTS

↑
Adam Wainwright (right) and his brother Trey Wainwright (left) at the 2011 Adam Wainwright Golf Classic.

"Show me the money!"

If you've seen the movie Jerry Maguire then you know what I'm talking about. I can see Cuba Gooding Jr. in my mind shouting that famous phrase while dancing in his kitchen.

In today's world of sports, money is the name of the game. Owners, managers, and players alike want you to "show them the money." Anything you can do as an athlete to get an advantage over your opponent is thought to be fair game — as long as you don't get caught.

Managers spend their entire careers stealing the signs of other coaches from the dugouts and down the baselines. Players who reach base often tell the hitter in the batter's box what pitch is coming after watching what number the catcher puts down.

As pitchers, we are supposed to throw clean, unscratched baseballs every pitch. A bounced ball can sometimes land a deep scuff that the umpire is supposed to check and throw away. A big league pitcher can do some pretty cool things with a scuffed baseball. A scuff on the right side of the ball will dive hard to the left, and a scuff on the left side will cause the ball to dive hard to the right.

So when we get a ball that has been bounced a few times we throw it back, right? Not in a million years. We know that the hitter is trying to beat us. We know that his manager is trying to steal our signs. We know that the runner on second base is trying to relay what pitch we're throwing. We know that the ball with the little scuff on the side is going to be much harder for the hitter to hit. And we know that by gaining that little edge over the hitter, we may have a greater opportunity to win the game, and by having a greater chance to win we know that we, potentially, have a chance to make more money.

And owners, managers, and players like money.

So we take that ball with the three-inch scratch and we throw it.

Now, most of those things are just traditions that are part of the great game of baseball. But, it makes you ask yourself, "Where do you draw the line?" That is what is so great about golf. The line is drawn right before you step onto the first tee box. While other sports all have referees watching your every move to ensure a fair game is played on both sides, the game of golf requires only one referee — yourself.

I believe the reason that golf has remained such a pure game is found at its roots. The game of golf is based on the values of honesty and a general understanding of what is right and what is wrong. The driving force behind golf's greatness is one little nine-letter word: integrity.

In the pages of this book, you will hear from some of today's top golfers who are not only known for their abilities on the course, but are equally known for their impeccable integrity. I've been privileged to interact with several PGA Tour athletes, including Jonathan Byrd, who have graciously participated in my annual FCA golf tournament on Sea Island, Georgia. I can think of no better examples from which we can all learn how to more passionately pursue Christ-like integrity.

As you read *Life in the Fairway*, I trust that you will be inspired and challenged to apply these biblical principles that will transform your hearts and ignite a deeper relationship with God.

Adam Wainwright signs autographs for the kids at the 2011 Adam Wainwright Golf Classic.

If you're not cheating, you're not trying.

That old adage is, at times, intended to be a tongue-in-cheek statement about the competitive nature of athletics. Unfortunately, it's become less of an exception and more often the rule at all levels — from grade school sports all the way up to the professional ranks.

In baseball, catchers pull an errant pitch back into the strike zone in an effort to sway the umpire's call. Outfielders trap fly balls after a diving attempt and quickly pop up to declare they made the catch. Base runners steal signs and relay the information to the base coach who then relays the information to the batter.

In football, offensive linemen invent techniques to help them get away with holding their defensive counterparts. Like baseball outfielders, receivers also trap the ball and do their best sales pitch to convince referees of a clean catch.

Basketball is equally notorious for producing a culture that encourages players to work around the rules. Defensive practices such as inconspicuously holding onto another player's shorts or jersey and flopping in order to draw a charge are commonplace mechanisms used to gain an unfair advantage.

And then there are more egregious forms of cheating such as the use of performance-enhancing drugs, the falsifying of birth certificates, and secretly videotaping another team's practice.

So why exactly has cheating become such a prominent factor in modern-day sports? There's an easy answer to that question: It's all about the big W. All too many owners, executives, coaches, and athletes have bought into a statement by UCLA Bruins' football coach Red Sanders that was later repeated and made famous by legendary Green Bay Packers' coach Vince Lombardi.

Winning isn't everything. It's the only thing.

Of course, it doesn't help that professional sports (and now even college sports) has become

such a big business. There are multi-million dollar contracts to be signed. There is power to be gained. There is fame in which to bask. There is personal pride and self-satisfaction to be enjoyed.

In many regards, golf is no different from those other sports. It can become a lucrative career for the elite athletes that reach the top. It can also bring varying levels of fame, power, and pleasure. But unlike baseball, football, basketball, and just about any other sport imaginable, golf has the concept of integrity tightly woven into its fabric. Golf makes you decide what kind of person you're going to be. Are you going to follow the rules regardless of the consequences or are you going to take advantage of the fact that in most situations, it's just you, your ball, and individual decisions that ultimately reflect how much you respect the game, your opponent, and yourself?

That's what this book is all about. It features some of the game's biggest stars sharing stories of tough decisions they've been forced to make on the golf course and in their personal lives. Sometimes the consequences were unfair. Other times, the end results worked out in their favor. But at no time did they waver from the biblically inspired integrity that they committed to pursuing once they entered into a relationship with Christ.

Throughout these pages, it is my prayer that you will gain a deeper understanding of integrity and why it still matters in this morally relativistic time in which we live. As Stewart Cink told me, "You've got trouble to the left and right every day now on these courses." That's why it's tougher and tougher for even the best pro golfers to keep their ball on the fairway.

The same is true in the life of the Christian. Our goal is to stay on the narrow road that Jesus talks about in Matthew 7:14. But in a world that favors pride over humility, lust over love, and selfishness over servitude, walking on the straight path has become an increasingly difficult task. Just like on the golf course, it can be all too easy to get lost in the rough, fall into a water hazard, or find ourselves out of bounds.

But with the truth found in God's Word, the corrective guidance of the Holy Spirit, and the accountability and support of like-minded individuals, we will discover that there is an abundance of true peace, prosperity, and purpose when we pursue *Life in the Fairway*.

The driving force behind integrity.

a love story

We don't mean to fall in love. It kind of just happens.

First, she catches our eye. And even though we're not looking for a new relationship, there's no denying this sudden feeling of excitement.

After working up the courage, we introduce ourselves and, if we're not careful, get caught up in an innocent game of flirtation. If we're lucky, the conversation grows deeper and we get the chance to spend some quality time together — and some more time after that, and even more time after that.

Before we know it, we're hooked. The bug has bitten. We're in love.

The relationship is by no means perfect, but during the honeymoon phase, it's easy to overlook the minor incompatibilities. It can be costly at times, too, but does true love have a price? Of course it doesn't.

But then a problem arises. We have our first fight. Those minor incompatibilities don't seem so minor anymore. Still, we vow to fight through the thoughts of discontent and through trial and error, we promise to do better. We want to make it work.

Then we hit the wall. We start asking ourselves some tough questions. Is this as good as it gets? Can this relationship really improve? Did we make a big mistake?

Golf

"Golf is always a challenge. It's different every day. It's you against the golf course. You can't blame anyone else. It's just your own performance. There are so many aspects to the game. You have the long shots and the chip shots and the bunker shots and the putting. It's all very different. Golf has the most wonderful rules and there's (the element) of integrity and honesty that comes with it. Golf was a great game to pursue when I was younger and I don't regret it today."

— Bernhard Langer

And then out of nowhere, it happens. We recapture that first moment and we're reminded why we fell in love in the first place. It doesn't mean the problems go away and it certainly doesn't make the work less arduous, but at least we have something to hold on to — a moment in time where everything is perfect. And that helps us make it through another day.

Depending on your perspective, these past few paragraphs could have been describing a marriage. Or maybe it was a metaphorical take on the game of golf. Perhaps it was a valid portrayal of both. Because let's face it — golf is a lot like marriage.

Perhaps that analogy is a bit simplistic. But looking at the genesis of any long-term relationship, the similarities between the game and matrimony start to add up.

At times it might seem that marriage, like golf, offers fewer highs than lows, more defeats than victories, and bigger steps backward than forward. But when the relationship is good, it's really good.

Like marriage, golf is impossible to perfect, yet we pursue perfection or at least the thought of inching closer to perfection with every swing. That's why for millions of us, golf tells a love story of sorts.

Even when the things that make us mad about the game can be downright maddening.

The Lure of History

For some professional golfers, the love of the game begins with golf's grandiose past and colorful folklore — not necessarily the ancient history that dates back (at least by most historians' accounts) to 15th-century Scotland, but rather its modern, 20th-century incarnation. Ask any of them what legendary golfer they most revere and the reaction will be quick and varied. Conversations about prestigious tournaments and difficult courses will invoke both expected and surprising responses.

Columbus, OH: This photograph of the Scioto Country Club was taken during a charitable golf tournament held on October 5, 1918. Citizens bid for the privilege to serve as walking caddies for the nationally known foursome of Chick Evans, National Open champion, and Elaine Rosenthal, Western Women's champion, playing against Bobby Jones, Southern champion, and Alexa Sterling, Women's Open champion. The event raised more than $6,500. UA Archives - Upper Arlington Public Library (Repository: UA Historical Society)

PGA golfer Aaron Baddeley was introduced to the game by his family, except it was his grandmothers, not his parents, who taught him at the age of eight how to maneuver the links. From there, Baddeley became obsessed with golf and followed its stars religiously.

"Growing up, I knew everyone, especially the big names," he recalls. "I watched so much golf it was ridiculous. I could tell you every shot Nick Price hit in the last round when he won the PGA at Southern Hills (in 1994). I could tell you the commentary. Ever since I started playing golf, I just loved watching it."[1]

Baddeley easily could have been star struck when he first played a PGA event in 2000, but somehow managed to avoid that common rookie scenario thanks to his previous experience playing with fellow Australian (and golf legend) Greg Norman. Even when his playing partner at the Masters was Tiger Woods, Baddeley remained calm and thoroughly enjoyed the moment.

"I wanted to go play," Baddeley says. "I wanted to show Tiger that I could play the game."[2]

Perhaps Baddeley might have been more nervous had he been given the opportunity to play with golf legend Ben Hogan in his prime. The same could be said for fellow PGA tour member D.J. Brigman who names Hogan as one of his historical favorites.

"There was a mystique about Ben Hogan," Brigman says. "I've heard so many stories growing up and playing at Shady Oaks. The stories are pretty incredible. I'd like to be able to see it in person."[3]

Hogan's 64 PGA wins and nine Major championships (including four U.S. Open titles) clearly make him one of the game's greats. But you have to go back to the 1920s and 1930s to find another endearing figure that has captured the imagination of today's best golfers: Bobby Jones.

←Bobby Jones

"Bobby Jones had such an incredible mind for the game," PGA golfer Ben Crane says. "He was at the top of the game as an amateur. He played for great reasons with great integrity and the instructional videos that he made are so spot on, so simple, yet the more we learn about golf and the swing, I think they were incredible lessons of fundamentals."[4]

Jones died before most of the current PGA players featured in this book were even born, yet his legacy continues to provide a backdrop for many of the reasons they love the game. Not only did he win seven Majors and a combined six amateur titles (five U.S., and one British), Jones also co-designed the hallowed Augusta National course and founded the Masters Tournament.

PGA golfer Stewart Cink appreciates all of those historical tidbits but enjoys some closer ties to the iconic golf legend.

"Bobby Jones was from Georgia Tech like me," Cink says. "He was a member at East Lake, which is also where my home course is located. I've got a lot of connections to him. He's kind of an enigma that no one really knows that much about. There's not a lot of video footage of him playing. We don't know much about him and he played with weird clubs. I'd like to see how he did what he did because he was the greatest of his era."[5]

From the National Library of Ireland 1880 – 1914 ↓

↑
Bobby Jones, Coolidge, July 21, 1921

Of course, much of the love does end up making its way back across the Atlantic Ocean to the Old Country, or to be more specific the United Kingdom, where classic links courses provide a playing experience like no other. Cink admits he didn't believe the hype at first.

"My first positive influence in the game was Chris Burns," he says. "Chris was a PGA member and the head pro at Florence Country Club for many years. He had a great respect for links golf over in Britain. He always told me they were the best and they had the best turf and everything was better over there than it was over here. I just thought he was full of it. Then I started playing in the British Open and as soon as I stepped foot on my first links course, I understood exactly what he was talking about."[6]

Crane can relate to Cink's enthusiastic approval. He lists the historic Old Course at St. Andrews in Scotland as his favorite place to play. Crane's strong affection for the nearly 500-year-old course (making it the oldest in the world) is in spite of its numerous blind tee shots — something Crane usually dislikes.

"Coming into that course and playing those greens, how firm they are no matter if its rainy or sunny, it just teaches you everything you want to know about playing golf," Crane says. "What a fantastic experience it was to play in the Open Championship (in 2010). I learned so much."[7]

Cink lists the famous 17th hole (also referred to as "the Road Hole") as both his favorite and toughest hole on which to play. An argument for the latter is much easier made than the former. Using a blind tee, golfers must aim over a corner of the Old Course Hotel. There's also a sand trap right in front of the green aptly named "Road Hole Bunker." And on the back side of the green there are multiple hazards, including a tarmac roadway and an old stone wall, both of which are in play.

"When you make the turn and the wind's just whipping, those holes are so challenging," Crane adds. "You have to play so many different shots just to fight the ball into the wind. It's just a fantastic course."[8]

The Love of a Challenge

Cink and Crane's enthusiastic endorsements of a course that inherently gives them fits showcases a quirky personality trait embedded deeply into the DNA of most every golfer from the amateur ranks up to the highest professional level: oh, how they love a challenge.

"Golf is a game that you will never master, but always try to," Baddeley simply but succinctly explains.[9]

Within that challenge is something that separates golf from the popular team sports that dominate Western culture. Baddeley refers to it as his "responsibility."[10] In other words, golf is a game that pits one individual against the course. Sure, there are other competitors in the field of play, but it really boils down to what each golfer can accomplish individually on any given day.

"I played team sports all my life growing up until I got to the age of 13 and then I got interested in golf," Brigman says. "I loved the individual aspect. It was all on myself and I couldn't put blame on anybody else. If I didn't perform well, I just accepted it and then I could do something

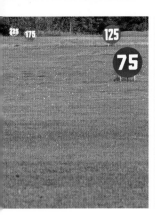

about it. The harder I worked and the more effort I put into it, the greater the benefits and improvement I saw in my game."[11]

Just like other individual sports such as tennis and track, golfers do employ a team of coaches, trainers, and even psychologists to help them achieve their best results. And on the course they have a caddie that helps them make crucial decisions regarding distance, wind conditions, and club selection.

But once the golfer approaches the shot, takes that stance, and starts into a backswing motion, it's between him, his club, the ball, and the hole in the ground that measures 4.25 inches in diameter. What happens next can be determined by numerous factors that invoke elements of the golfer's physical, mental, and emotional state. We'll hear more about that in another chapter and find out what constitutes the perfect swing, but one thing is for sure: golf is a game where small things make a big difference and the challenge for all golfers is finding out how to turn small changes into big results.

"It doesn't take much in golf," Brigman says. "One day can be completely different from the next. It just takes a small fraction of an inch for a shot to go awry. But when you do hit those shots that go exactly where you want them to go, it just seems magical."[12]

Brigman describes those moments as "hitting the sweet spot."[13] When he started playing as a 13 year old growing up in New Mexico, he admits most of his shots at the driving range were "tops or skulls or slices or hooks."[14]

"Then I'd hit that one that hit the sweet spot and it went straight as an arrow and I didn't know how I did it but hitting that one shot kept bringing me back," Brigman says. "I'd go home after practicing on the range and I'd remember that shot until the next time. That kept drawing me back to the sport."[15]

The Quest for Perfection

Crane had a similar experience as a young golfer. He spent countless hours at the Portland Golf Club in his hometown of Portland, Oregon, working on his putting stroke. A little light that hung from the side of the clubhouse was just bright enough to expose one or two of the putting green's holes. Crane would usually spend at least two hours there each night from about 9 until 11 o'clock.

"My goal was to make 100 three-footers in a row and if I did that, I could go home," he says. "But if I got to 99 and missed, I'd start over. That happened a few times, which was frustrating, but it's one of the reasons why I've grown to become a good putter."[16]

Brigman too has found himself obsessing over perfection. No longer good enough is that feeling of elation he experienced when hitting a single good shot. It takes so much more to satisfy his cravings these days.

"It's funny, as a professional, I probably hit about 98 or 99 percent of my shots in the sweet spot, but I focus most of my energy on that one shot that I don't hit as well. That's the quest for perfection as I try to get all my shots where I want them. My mentality has shifted, which is kind of silly."[17]

Silly or not, Crane and Brigman are stereotypical of how elite golfers approach the game. And while the desire to achieve flawless excellence on the course can be maddening, it nonetheless wields a significant magnetic pull on those who dare to take on the challenge.

"Golf is so difficult to master," Cink explains. "It feels like the better you get, the further you are away from perfection. A beginner gets so excited when he hits the ball in the air or maybe hits a nice bunker shot. A player who has won major championships doesn't get that excited about those shots anymore. It takes a lot more to excite you. The closer you get to perfection, the more difficult it becomes."[18]

The Ultimate Love Story

The golfer's quest for perfection sounds a lot like another journey upon which many have embarked. It could easily be described as the most difficult, if not impossible, goal set before mankind not by the PGA, the USGA, or golfers of any skill level, but rather by our Creator.

In Matthew 5:48, Jesus made this profound statement: "Be perfect, therefore, as your heavenly Father is perfect."

By most theological accounts, the person who made that statement is the only person who can lay claim to successfully achieving its command. That's because only Jesus was born as the Son of God and only Jesus lived a perfect, sinless life. But yet, there it is written plainly for all to read: "Be perfect."

Transferring that command to the golf course seems to be quite a stretch as well, although it's been tried many times over.

"You start out every round with an opportunity to be perfect," Brigman says. "You try to stay as perfect as you can for as long as possible. A lot of people say perfect is a 59 or a 58 or a 54.

Everyone has an opinion of what perfection is. It might be making no bogies or hitting every fairway and every green and averaging 1.5 putts per green. The mere possibility is something that keeps me coming back. I look at a round of golf and see the mistakes that I made and I practice those areas so I can eliminate those mistakes the next day."[19]

Likewise, Brigman says that the life of a Christian, one who follows the teachings of Jesus and has called upon Him as his or her Savior from all sins, is all about striving for that seemingly impossible perfection that Jesus talked about.

"Perfection might be going throughout your day without sinning," Brigman opines. "We know that's fleeting and it will never happen, but we still strive for that. As a Christian, you look back on your day and say your prayers at night and ask God for forgiveness. The next day, you want to handle those opportunities differently. Knowing that I'm never going to be perfect but striving for that is something that keeps me going and keeps me motivated."[20]

For Brigman, Baddeley, Cink, Crane, and other golfers featured in this book, the desire to follow Christ's command in Matthew 5:48 is fortified by a teaching found in the Apostle Paul's writings. Ephesians 5:1 lays out a blueprint for perfection when it says we should, "Be imitators of God" (NASB).

We'll talk more about what it looks like to imitate God (as exemplified by the life of Christ) in the final chapter and we'll get some examples of what integrity looks like from the perspective of PGA golfers like Jonathan Byrd, Stewart Cink, and Webb Simpson. But for now, let's just say the best way to achieve perfection (or at least the closest thing humanly possible) is to do as Christ did and live a life that seeks to do everything with integrity — whether that means loving others selflessly, resisting the many temptations that cross our path, setting an example for others, or living the same way in private as we do in public.

Jesus set that example of integrity for us because He loves us. In fact, the Bible says in Ephesians 5:25 that "Christ also loved the church" in the same way that husbands are called to love their wives. He wanted to show us the best way to live and how we can steer clear of the traps that might destroy us should we live absent of biblical integrity.

And when we truly love Him, we will want to be like Him. It won't be about following the rules or making sure we stay out of trouble. It won't be inspired by an appreciation of the Bible and its historical relevancy. And it certainly won't be or the love of the challenge or for the futile quest for perfection.

No, instead, our love for God will create a strong desire to live like we love Him—simply because "He first loved us" (1 John 4:19).

That is the ultimate love story.

Integrity Has No Regrets.

Jonathan

Jonathan Byrd was frustrated.

It's a common occurrence experienced by golfers at every level, and the big name professionals on the PGA Tour are by no means exempt. But during the first round at the 2005 Reno-Tahoe Open, Byrd admittedly let his internal dissatisfaction get the best of him. After missing a make-able putt, he approached the short tap-in quicker than usual. He intended to "jab it in the hole" when something peculiar happened. Byrd lost his balance. And then, something even stranger happened. While attempting to hit the ball, he made a sub-conscious decision to pull back.

It was too late. Byrd whiffed the shot. Before anyone had a chance to notice, he instinctively reset his stance and tapped the ball in the hole.

"At the moment I was thinking I didn't hit the ball and I didn't think it was an infraction," Byrd says. "I was uncertain if I really made a swing at it because it was so awkward. It was just a weird thing. I was just thinking, *Nah, that wasn't that big of a deal. I didn't intend to hit it.*"[1]

Byrd finished the round with an even par score of 72. He signed his scorecard and headed back to the hotel room. By then, Byrd was starting to struggle with the events surrounding his mis-hap on the green. He was uncertain of his intention. If Byrd had intended to strike the ball but completely missed, he knew it should have been a one-stroke penalty, and a penalty cannot be

Byrd

"After a bad round where other guys might have gotten angry or lost it, I've been able to keep my composure and I've had people come up to me and ask, 'What's the difference? Why didn't you act the other way?'"

— Jonathan Byrd

added retroactively to a player's score. Therefore, Byrd had a difficult question to answer: Was he trying to strike the ball or not?

In the end, Byrd's integrity and his desire to live free of regrets was the most important factor as he decided how to proceed.

"To be honest, it was 50-50," Byrd recalls. "In the rulebook, it says that if there's any doubt in the player's mind, then it goes against the player. So the next morning, I went to the course early and I grabbed an official. I broke it down for him and told him what happened. It was still a gray area. But I felt like it was better not to play if there was doubt in my mind and I withdrew from the tournament."[2]

The Best Policy

You might think that part in the rulebook that places the onus on the golfer would be one of Byrd's least favorite things about golf. After all, in the situation at the Reno-Tahoe Open, Byrd's adherence to the principle cost him a shot at making the cut and a paycheck worth a few thousand dollars. But in fact, it's those built-in accountabilities that make him love the game even more.

Byrd loves the game for other reasons, too, like the simple allure of its natural setting and the relational aspect of playing alongside other golfers and interacting with officials, sponsors, and fans.

Jonathan & wife Amanda ↓

"If you're out there playing for four or five hours, you're only hitting the ball for about an hour of that time," he says. "The rest of the time you're interacting with people. It's a great game."[3]

That's partly why Byrd now takes his son Jackson to play golf just like his father once took him. But there are some even more important reasons why he wants to pass the game along to the next generation.

"You can teach your son a lot about respect through the rules of the game, how you should treat your playing partner, how you can encourage the other player when they hit a good shot," Byrd says. "I'm excited about that for my son because you can teach many life lessons about how to interact with people and how to have integrity by following the rules of the game."[4]

↑

Jonathan & his son Jackson

Perhaps paramount among those lessons that golf teaches is the simple, yet often under-appreciated principle of honesty. Byrd admits that when he was a young golfer, he struggled with that notion — especially when keeping his own score and sometimes his playing partner's score. But eventually, the biblically inspired concept hit home. If he made a five, he had to write down a five. If he made a six, he had to write down a six. It didn't matter how painful it was at the time, if Byrd shot poorly on a hole, he had to be honest — even if he was playing by himself.

It might be cliché, but honesty really is the best policy. It is one of the first defenses against regret. In fact, King Solomon gives quite a bit of solid advice on the matter including Proverbs 19:1 where he writes, "Better a poor man whose walk is blameless than a fool whose lips are perverse. " Why, you ask? Because, "A false witness will not go unpunished, and he who pours out lies will not go free" (Proverbs 19:5).

And while Byrd doesn't live in fear of making mistakes, he is keenly aware of the fact that there's nothing anyone can hide from the Creator. "Obviously God knows our thoughts," he says. "He knows everything that we do."[5]

Humility Has Its Ways

Like all professional sports, golf is a game that affords the average competitor more failure than success. Of course, even the least successful players on the PGA do all right for themselves. Gregory Havret, for instance, finished 250th on the 2011 Money List after playing three events and secured just over $71,000 in the process.[6] That's $17,000 more than the average household income for the same year.[7]

Still, Byrd says that humility has its ways of keeping him and others on the Tour from getting complacent or even too prideful about whatever successes they might experience. Through 2011 (Byrd's 10th year on the PGA Tour), he had won five tournaments, which isn't a whole lot compared to some other sports. That sobering reality helps him keep his head both out of the clouds and out of the sand.

"There's nothing that humbles you more than the game of golf," Byrd says. "It can really humble you sometimes and having a bad golf score can teach you a lot about pride. The minute you think you have the game figured out and you become boastful about it, the game will humble you right around the corner and you'll struggle."[8]

"But the standard for winning or improvement and things like that is also very important to help you deal with defeat," he adds. "We obviously play to win tournaments. We practice a lot. But when we're struggling and we're not playing well, the thing that keeps bringing me back is the fact that I can always improve on something. It's a game you can't perfect. But the pursuit of perfection is very fun. I love working with my instructor and figuring things out that might make me better and then trying to ingrain that through the drills and putting the time and seeing the fruit of that. It's just a real enjoyable process."[9]

Byrd has found that the impossible task of perfecting his game is much like the even more difficult quest for perfection as a Christian. He is humbled when he thinks about how Christ lived a sinless life compared to the spiritual challenges he faces every day.

"We're called to be a light," Byrd says. "We're called to live like Christ and be like Christ. But we can't do it through our own strength. It's impossible. I am a sinful, fallen man. Christ called us to not just look at our actions but to look at our thoughts. If people could see my thoughts, they'd know I'm an extremely fallen man. You fall so short but it's good to have a standard of perfection. Jesus is the way, the truth, and the life. The more we trust Him, the more we understand Him. The more we pursue the things of God, the more we realize that He's worthy of our trust. That's when we're on the right path and on the right pursuit."[10]

Train a Child

Byrd doesn't just experience humility as a golfer and as a Christian. He gets heavy doses of the stuff from his role as a father. He doesn't claim to be the perfect dad nor does he worry too much about it. Instead, Byrd tries to do his best to live the wisdom of Proverbs 22:6: "Train a child in the way he should go, and when he is old he will not turn from it."

Jackson & Caroline

"As the spiritual leader of my family as a husband and as a father, I am an example to them through how I live my life," Byrd says. "I can be a good example or a bad example. I can model to my kids how I love their mom and how I submit to God's authority. My kids aren't going to submit to me as their father if they don't see me submitting to God. That doesn't jive with kids. When I screw up and I come to them and ask for their forgiveness, those are some of the sweetest times I've had with my kids. That's also modeled in the things I do well like when they see me reading the Bible, when they see me praying, or when they see me treating someone with respect."[11]

Fatherhood also gives Byrd ample opportunity to clearly differentiate between the satisfaction that comes from living with integrity and the regret that accompanies making poor decisions. When his son Jackson was five years old, Byrd says that his wife Amanda "got fired up" one day due to some naughty behavior.

"She was just tired as mommies can get and she yelled at him," Byrd recalls. "Amanda felt like after the situation was over that she shouldn't have yelled at him. So she went into his room and wrote on piece of paper that she was sorry and she wanted him to forgive her. Then she put it on his door in his room."[12]

A few days later, the tables were turned and Jackson got mad at his mother and yelled at her. She promptly sent him to his room where he finally noticed that note pinned to the door.

"After a little while, Jackson came to her and said, 'Hey, Mommy, I just want to say I'm sorry,' and he asked her for forgiveness," Byrd says. "It was just so cool."[13]

It might seem contradictory, but there are two iconic Bible verses that address this very common scenario that all parents face at one time or another. In Ephesians 6:4, the Apostle Paul advises parents to "provoke not your children to wrath: but bring them up in the nurture and admonition of the Lord" (KJV). But in Proverbs 13:24, Solomon writes, "Those who spare the rod of discipline hate their children. Those who love their children care enough to discipline them" (NLT).

Young Jonathan

Byrd Boys:
Jonathan (left),
father Jim, and
brother Jordan

In reality, these two Scriptures work perfectly together. Parents shouldn't anger or (as the New International Version puts it) exasperate their children with sporadic and inconsistent discipline. But correction and encouragement should work together to help bring them to a better understanding of who God is and why obedience is in their best interest. The overbearing parent will push their child away while the lenient parent will lose control of their child by giving up authority. Certainly both of these scenarios will bring both emotional distress and heartbreaking regret.

And just as he approaches his golf game and his walk with God, Byrd says the pursuit of integrity as a father and a husband always boils down to trust. Even though he admits that Proverbs 3:5–6 is "grossly overused in sports,"[14] it contains a powerful application: "Trust in the Lord with all your heart and lean not on your own understanding; in all your ways acknowledge him, and he will make your paths straight."

"A lot of times, people in sports use that passage to say, 'Trust the Lord and He'll make things right for me. He'll help me win,'" Byrd says. "But I think it means we're supposed to trust the Lord with everything. I'm bombarded every day with situations where God asks, 'Are you going to trust Me?' And by that, He's saying, 'Trust me with this difficult relationship' and 'Trust me with this financial decision.' "[15]

That Scripture especially challenged Byrd in 2009 when his father Jim passed away after a difficult battle with brain cancer. It was his father who had taught him the game of golf and was so influential in his understanding of integrity.

"The part about not leaning on my own understanding really grips me," Byrd says. "In my mind, it doesn't make sense. It didn't make sense when my dad died. Why did that happen? It was something I struggled to understand. So I have to continually and daily, with little things that dig at me, trust God. That is the only way to live. Any other way is futile."[16]

Excess Baggage

When Byrd hits the course, his caddy must make sure to accurately count how many clubs are in the golf bag. Rule 4-4 in the USGA's "Rules of Golf" states that "The player must not start a stipulated round with more than fourteen clubs." In stroke play, the players will receive a two-stroke penalty "for each hole at which any breach occurred" with a maximum penalty per round of four strokes.[17]

In other words, excess baggage can be costly.

It's hard to imagine the kind of regret a caddy might experience if his mistake cost the golfer a chance to make the cut, finish in the top 25, or even win the whole tournament. But that's not the only kind of baggage the professional golfer must be wary of before heading to the first tee box.

"You don't want to have a heavy heart," Byrd says. "If things are unresolved with relationships, we need to make it right — to confess quickly and to repent quickly and daily and make things right. Doing that with my wife is great for my marriage. When I've screwed up and when I'm in the wrong, I need to ask for forgiveness and then move on."[18]

Byrd's concept of either asking forgiveness or accepting forgiveness (depending on the circumstance) is rooted in God's Word. In James 5:16, the Apostle writes, "Therefore confess your sins to each other and pray for each other so that you may be healed." Many have interpreted that Scripture to mean that prayers will remain unanswered until forgiveness has taken place. But there's another possible application here. Healing isn't always in the physical body. Sometimes healing needs to take place in the mind and in the spirit. And according to James, this won't occur until unfinished business has been settled through the confession and forgiveness of sin. In other words, our effectiveness in various aspects of our lives can often be hindered if we fail to ask for forgiveness or if we fail to forgive those who have hurt us in some way.

"On the golf course, the only person that hurts is you," Byrd says. "It's obviously not going to impact your competition. They don't know what's going on. They're going to play independently. When you're carrying heavy burdens that you're not meant to carry, it's going to hurt you. It might hurt your golf. It might hurt your marriage. You never know how it can impact you."[19]

There's also the excess baggage that comes from regrets related to our relationship with God. Byrd knows that hidden sin will eventually catch up to him. And in the meantime, it will weigh him down and keep him from fulfilling his potential and his purpose. That's why the admonition of Hebrews 12:1 is so important. It reminds us to "throw off everything that hinders and the sin that so easily entangles."

"If I need to repent or confess my sins to God or someone else, I need to do that and move on and not feel guilty and keep moving on and keep pursuing God," Byrd says. "I need to do that with golf, with life, with my marriage, and with my kids."[20]

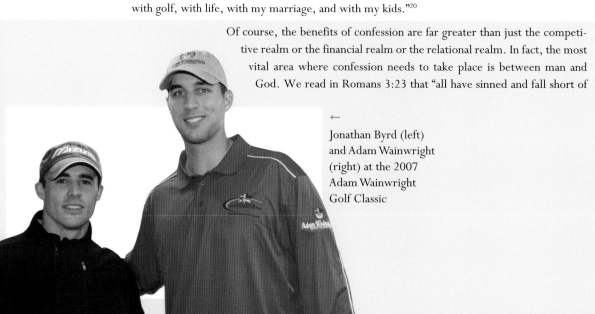

Of course, the benefits of confession are far greater than just the competitive realm or the financial realm or the relational realm. In fact, the most vital area where confession needs to take place is between man and God. We read in Romans 3:23 that "all have sinned and fall short of

←
Jonathan Byrd (left)
and Adam Wainwright
(right) at the 2007
Adam Wainwright
Golf Classic

the glory God." This of course is a result of Adam and Eve's disobedience in the Garden of Eden (Genesis 3), but thankfully was rectified by the crucifixion of Christ (Matthew 27), which gave all of mankind the opportunity to be saved from their sins.

Then, living without regrets becomes a choice. As the Apostle John writes in 1 John 1:9, "If we confess our sins, he is faithful and just and will forgive us our sins and purify us from all righteousness." And then we can have access to the "peace of God, which transcends all understanding" (Philippians 4:7).

"There's no better feeling than to have peace on the golf course — to know that your finances are in order, your marriage is in order, your kids are in good shape, your relationships are good," Byrd says. "All of those things give you freedom to play better golf and more importantly to walk confidently knowing that God can use you for His purpose."[21]

BACK 9

1	What's your favorite thing about golf?	It's being able to work on a part of the game and then go implement it and see the improvement during competition when you're under pressure.
2	What's your least favorite thing about golf?	It's such a difficult game of ups and downs. You can't have any expectations.
3	What's your favorite golf course?	Carnoustie (Golf Club in Carnoustie, Angus, Scotland).
4	What's your favorite tournament?	The Masters.
5	What's your favorite hole?	The 18th hole at Pebble Beach. You get on that hole on a pretty day and it just doesn't get any better. It's like being a kid in a candy store.
6	What's the toughest hole you've ever played?	The last hole on Friday at a tournament where I'm trying to make the cut.
7	What's your favorite club?	My putter.
8	Who is your favorite playing partner?	David Toms. I always play well with him.
9	With what legend in their prime would you most enjoy playing 18 holes?	Ben Hogan.

SCORECARD

Birthdate	January 27, 1978
Birthplace	Anderson, SC
Residence	St. Simons Island, GA
College	Clemson (2000, Marketing)
Nationwide Tour Victories	1 (2001 BUY.COM Charity Pro-Am at The Cliffs)
PGA Tour wins	5 (2002 Buick Challenge, 2004 B.C. Open, 2007 John Deere Classic, 2010 Justin Timberlake Shriners Hospitals for Children Open, 2011 Hyundai Tournament of Champions)
Top 25 finishes	81
Top 10 finishes	35
Career PGA Tour money	$14,868,549

All stats through the 2011 season

→
Jonathan Byrd speaks
to participants of the
2008 Adam Wainwright
Golf Classic

A tradition of integrity.

history of

Dozens if not hundreds of lengthy books have been written about the history of golf. *Life in the Fairway* isn't meant to be that kind of work, but it still seems appropriate to take a look into the fascinating transformation that the game has gone through since its earliest beginnings.

Ask the average golf fan where the game originated and answers like England or more specifically Scotland will likely be offered. Certainly the Scots are often credited for birthing golf as we know it today, but the game's roots go much deeper and much further back in history.

For instance, the Roman Legion played a game at the time of Christ called Paganica. It was a stick and ball game that utilized a leather-covered ball stuffed with feathers.[1] Around a.d. 423, historical records reveal the emergence of a Chinese game called bu da.

"Bu Da is Chinese for 'hit, walk,'" golf historian and educator Gary Wiren says. "Sounds like golf to me."[2]

As the Eastern Roman Empire spread across Europe throughout the Middle Ages, various stick and ball games grew in popularity in what is now Germany, France, and the low countries. There was also a great deal of trade taking place between burgeoning regions such as Holland and the east coast of Scotland. From the 1300s, historians note depictions of the Dutch playing a game called "kolf" or "colf." Playing with sticks that resembled golf clubs, they used the ice as a

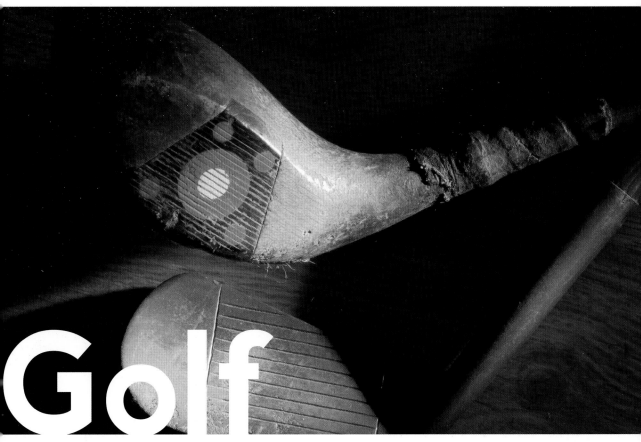

Golf

"Golf has taught me that if you're not practicing integrity in everything you're doing, you're cheating yourself in the long run. That translates into real life. When you go out there and do what's right on the golf course and you carry it over to your normal life, then you can hold your head high and look at yourself in the mirror and know that you're doing what is right."

— D.J. Brigman

surface during the winter and played in the fields during the summer. Wiren theorizes that the Scots may have picked up the game from the Dutch.[3]

"Golf as we know it emerged in the early 15th century, late 14th century in Scotland," USGA Senior Managing Director of Public Affairs Rand Jerris adds. "It's closest relatives were games that were played in the low countries and those sailors brought their games with them on the trade ships up to the east coast of Scotland."[4]

The Scots Parliament of King James II, however, banned the game because it was deemed a threat to the nation's security — the concern being that the young men of the kingdom were spending too much time playing golf, and not enough time practicing archery. The attempt to ban the game proved ineffective, and its popularity continued to grow throughout the British Isles. However, it wasn't for another 200 years or so, around the 1740s, when the rules of golf began to take shape and the oldest known code of rules was compiled for the Honourable Company of Edinburgh Golfers.[5]

Four gentlemen golfers on the tee of a golf course, circa 1930s.

Mrs. Gardiner and her daughter, Janet, play off in a golf final in Brisbane, Queensland, Australia.

"We've seen a lot of change in equipment," Jerris says. "We've seen a tremendous change in the social structures that surround the game. But if you were to read the rules from back then, you'd see that the fundamental principles are the same as the game we play today."[6]

And despite times in golf's history when the game wasn't inclusive to all social groups, genders, or races of people, one thing has remained the same. Integrity is the core principle that golf relies upon for its very existence.

"Playing the ball as you find it. Treating the course and your opponent and the game with respect. Those are all critical aspects of what makes the game so popular and so successful," Jerris says. "Integrity is a perfect word to associate with golf."[7]

Mr. Clampett and Mr. Downes with their juvenile caddies at Tramore Golf Links, Co. Waterford, Ireland, 1907.

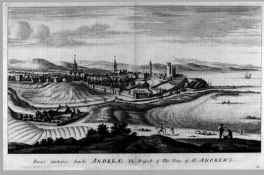

'The Prospect of the Town of St Andrews' from Theatrum Scotiae by John Slezer, 1693. The Society of St. Andrews Golfers was founded in 1754.

Integrity Has No Price.

Webb

A lot of things go through a golfer's mind before a crucial putt.

Are my hands in the right position?

Do I like my line?

How's my stance?

I wonder why they're cheering on the 18th?

Relax.

Visualize your swing.

And then, even if for just a split second, the most disciplined golfers empty them out and turn their laser-like focus onto the ball, the club, and the cup. As soon as the putter makes contact with the ball, one last thought fills the cranium.

Get in the hole!

Webb Simpson is no different than any other golfer. He has his routine. He has his progression. He has his collection of thoughts that race through his mind.

So when Simpson approached his ball on the 15th hole during the final round of the 2011 Zurich

Simpson

"You can play video games or board games or card games and it always seems like you can beat the game or perfect it. Well, in golf, you can never perfect it. The lowest round I ever shot was 58 and I felt like I left two shots out there. I missed a six-foot putt on one hole and I made par on a par five that was reachable. So I think that element of thinking you can always do better is what keeps people coming back whether they're an amateur or a professional."

-- Webb Simpson

Classic, like clockwork, he did the same thing he always does. Only this time, the stakes were much higher. Tapping in this six-inch putt meant that just three more holes would separate Simpson from his first career PGA Tour victory.

Up until that Sunday in Avondale, Louisiana, a suburb just 15 miles west of New Orleans, the Wake Forest All-American had managed to make a modest impact on the circuit. He was winless, but four Top-10 finishes had helped the rookie place 70th on the 2010 money list. Earlier in the 2011 season, Simpson had his first close call at the Transitions Championship before a bogey on the final hole knocked him out of a first-place tie with Gary Woodland.[1]

Other than the unusually high winds of 17 miles per hour (as opposed to the average 9 mph typical of late April and early May),[2] it was an uneventful sunny spring day in the Gulf Coast. Players especially needed to make adjustments on their tee shots and approaches, but for the most part weren't as concerned about the weather condition's impact on the putting game.

Simpson certainly didn't hold a lackadaisical attitude. He knew anything was possible as he paced a green that he would later describe as "pretty bare."[3] The lanky 6' 2" Raleigh, North Carolina, native approached the ball, took his stance, set his feet, and grounded his putter six inches behind the ball.

And then, just as he was ready to pull back his club and make contact, Simpson's ball moved.

Oh no. Not again.

It wasn't more than a half-inch, but it moved nonetheless.

For Simpson, that singular moment felt like part déjà vu and part nightmare. He was instantly transported back in time to the 2009 Bob Hope Classic where on the 11th hole of the final round he experienced the same agonizing circumstances. The wind moved his ball after he had addressed the ball and grounded his club, resulting in a one-stroke penalty. Simpson finished that tournament tied for fifth.[4]

"If you address the ball with the intention of making a stroke and the ball moves, you're deemed to have caused it to move," Simpson explains. "If the ball is there and you put your putter down but you haven't set your feet in place and it moves, that's no big deal. But if you're ready to putt and your next step is to take your putter back, then that's a penalty."[5]

Simpson knew the ball moved, but apparently he was the only who actually saw it move. Still, in his mind, there was only one choice: go to the officials and ask if he had taken his stance. After conferring about the situation, they ruled that he had, in fact, taken his stance. Instead of a par four to keep him in the lead by a stroke, Simpson made bogey on the hole and fell back into a tie with final round playing partner Bubba Watson.

"In the moment, it was tough," Simpson admits. "You're out there grinding and you're fighting and you're trying to win your first golf tournament, and you hate to think that might cause you to lose the tournament."[6]

Simpson didn't lose the tournament at that moment, but considering that he and Watson both went on to par the remaining three holes to force a sudden death playoff where Watson won on the second hole, some would argue that the penalty did in fact cost him the victory. If that's true, then the penalty also cost Simpson $460,800 — the difference between the first and second-place checks.[7]

Taking that logic one step further, it could be argued that the penalty eventually cost him much more. Nearly six months later, Simpson finished the 2011 season in second place on the money list with $6,347,353 behind Luke Donald who earned $6,683,214.[8] That's a difference of $335,861 or, more importantly, less than the $460,800 that Simpson didn't collect by falling short at the Zurich Classic. And with the money title comes a valuable five-year PGA Tour exemption.

As far as Simpson is concerned, integrity has no price. Simpson wasn't thinking about losing out on nearly half a million dollars and he certainly wasn't thinking about the impact it might have on his year-end stats. But in that moment, all he could think about was doing the right thing no matter how unfair the rule might have seemed at the time.

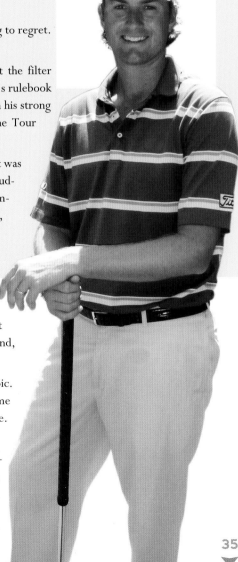

At the end of the tournament and having a moment to decompress, he turned to his wife Dowd for counsel. "I'm going to say what I think about this rule in the media room," he told her. "Do you think I should?"

"Yes," she replied. "But make sure you don't say anything you're going to regret. Do it in a way that still honors the Lord."[9]

Simpson went into the pressroom where he uncharacteristically "let the filter down."[10] While complimentary of the United States Golf Association's rulebook and showing his overall respect for its purpose, he didn't hold back on his strong opinion of this particular rule and his belief that every golfer on the Tour would agree that it was a rule that unfairly penalized competitors.

One of those peers that wholeheartedly supported Simpson's argument was American golfing legend Tom Lehman, a five-time PGA winner (including the 1996 British Open) and currently a dominant force on the Champions Tour. When Lehman watched the events unfold in New Orleans, he was immediately struck by not just the injustice of the situation but by how professionally and maturely Simpson handled himself in the aftermath.

"When you're in a position where it could cost you a tournament, it just shows the class, the integrity and the character of the individual and also the beauty of golf," Lehman says. "Webb paid the penalty. But you know what, I think in the end, when you do that, what goes around, comes around. He will be rewarded in some way."[11]

Simpson, however, doesn't feel like his decision was all that heroic. "I think and I hope that every other player would have done the same thing," he says. "It wasn't a choice that I had. It was a rule of the game. I've received too many compliments for just following the rules."[12]

Other golfers see it a little differently. Simpson's actions that day impressed several of his more experienced tour mates. Stewart Cink, Jonathan Byrd, Ben Crane, and close friend Kevin Streelman are all on record showing their admiration for his show of integrity. D.J.

Brigman, another rising star on the Tour, calls Simpson "a perfect example of integrity"[13] after watching him handle multiple situations when he could have easily made a more selfish decision.

"He did what was right," Brigman says. "It just speaks volumes to Webb's integrity and how his faith plays a part in his life. That will allow people to be open to what he has to say when it comes to his faith. He's going to be able to reach more people because of what he's done in those situations as opposed to winning those tournaments if he had done the wrong thing."[14]

Nudges in the Right Direction

Simpson didn't wake up on the morning of May 1, 2011, and suddenly have the moral fortitude to make a principled decision. The ability to make that tough call was seeded into his young heart and mind at home years earlier. He vividly remembers one time in particular when as a youngster his father taught him a lesson about integrity. Standing on the 18th fairway of a local golf course, nine-year-old Simpson noticed that there was a divot about a foot in front of dad's ball. At the time, there seemed to be an obvious opportunity. "Why don't you just tee it up on the front of that divot?" Simpson innocently asked.

"That would be closer to the hole," his father replied. "It doesn't matter if it's one inch, you can never, ever fib on the rules at all."[15]

Early on, it was teachable moments seized upon by his father that nudged him toward an appreciation for the value of honesty and ethical behavior. But as he grew older, Simpson began developing not only a strong love for golf, but a respect for the game as well. Those two powerful components have guided him throughout his amateur and professional careers — even when faced with seemingly unfair circumstances.

"If your ball moves a quarter of an inch or you ground the club in the sand and it barely touches the ball, you've always got to maintain the integrity of the game," Simpson says. "I've always remembered what my father taught me and it's helped me in those situations where nobody's looking and I'm the only one that knows that the ball moved. It has allowed me to keep the integrity of the game."[16]

One of Simpson's first major opportunities to test his adherence to that standard came in 2005 while playing at the College All-America Golf Classic in El Paso, Texas. Simpson entered his sophomore season with high expectations, having won Atlantic Coast Conference (ACC) Freshman of the Year honors just a few months earlier.[17]

Playing at the All-America tournament may not have been the Masters, but for Simpson and the 30-plus college golfers invited to play there, it probably seemed that big. The event has produced some notable winners such as Tiger Woods, Matt Kucher, and Davis Love III.[18]

During an early round, Simpson was working out of the rough. When he put down his club, the ball moved ever so slightly.

Did it move and come back to the original spot or did it move and stay there?

It was quite the conundrum for a young player eager to perform well on a sizable stage but equally fervent in his quest to maintain integrity. Simpson struggled with his decision. Thinking he could call a penalty on himself at the end of the round, he waited until entering the clubhouse before coming to a conclusion.

Turned out, Simpson was supposed to replace the ball if it had moved into a different position and then play his next shot.

"Either it moved and you're disqualified or it didn't move and you're fine," the officials informed him.

"I just kind of prayed about it," Simpson recalls. "I felt the Lord telling me to penalize myself. I did, and I got disqualified. It was really tough at the time because it was a huge tournament and a great honor to be there."[19]

Simpson wasn't able to play in El Paso the next year due to an injury, but returned in 2007 during his senior year where he claimed the prestigious title in redemptive fashion. "In no way am I suggesting I won because the Lord was rewarding me," Simpson clarifies. "But it was cool how I went through a difficult situation and then was able to win the golf tournament a couple years later."[20]

Simpson can think of at least ten times in his playing career where he faced a difficult decision involving a self-imposed penalty. But it ultimately wasn't the game that required him to act with integrity but rather his relationship with God and some timely nudges in the right direction.

"Our deposit of the Holy Spirit living inside of us, more than anything, has allowed me to make those tough decisions," Simpson says. "For me, it's not as much the nature of the game but the fact that the Holy Spirit is prompting me to call a penalty on myself. Within our own nature, we don't want to call a penalty on ourselves. We want to see how much we can get away with. That's been a part of every tough decision I've made in golf."[21]

Course Correction

For the golfer out on the course, the closest human equivalent to the Holy Spirit is his caddy. Of the caddy's numerous responsibilities, carrying the golfer's bag is probably one of the least important. The best caddies are intricately involved with virtually every shot a golfer takes. The caddy helps the player make sound decisions (what club to use, what type of shot to hit, etc.) based on natural elements such as the wind and the distance to the hole, along with his knowledge of the golfer's strengths, weaknesses, and ball-striking tendencies.

It's not uncommon for a golfer to have multiple caddies over the course of a sustained career, but preferably, it's nice to have the same person on your bag for an extended period of time. Bernhard Langer, for instance, worked with caddy Peter Coleman for 22 years before the two amicably parted ways.[22] When two people work together that long or even for 5 to 10 consecutive years, there's an ironclad trust that goes well beyond the golf course and carries over into their personal lives.

Simpson, on the other hand, has mostly worked with two caddies in his young career. The first was William Kane, who grew up with Simpson in Raleigh. Kane and Simpson became friends at the age of six while playing on the same youth basketball team. When Simpson pursued golf, Kane stuck with basketball and played at a small college. The two eventually reunited when Simpson joined the PGA Tour in 2009.[23]

But in 2010, Kane was diagnosed with multifocal motor neuropathy (MMN), a condition that is often confused with amyotrophic lateral sclerosis (ALS). In a day and age where performance is money, Simpson refused to turn his back on Kane and kept him on the bag until his good friend accepted an offer to go back into youth ministry.[24]

"Loyalty is one of the most important things, if not the number one thing, in a friendship, and that trust factor," Simpson says. "I think they go hand in hand."[25]

Needing a quick but solid replacement, Simpson was referred to veteran Paul Tesori by fellow PGA golfer and friend Nick Watney. Tesori had previously worked with Vijay Singh, Sean O'Hair, and Jerry Kelly, and was entertaining some high profile offers at the time. But after a ten-minute phone conversation, both men were sold and a new relationship was forged.[26]

Simpson and Tesori shared more than a love of golf and a collective vast knowledge of the game. They quickly learned that both were followers of Christ and have often relied on their faith to deal with daily challenges. Simpson was also immediately impressed by Tesori's professional and personal integrity.

"If he's thinking something, he's going to tell me," Simpson says. "He got a job offer (during the 2011 season) from a player who at the time was ranked way ahead of me. On paper, this player has had a way better career. (Paul) told me as soon as he got the voice mail from the guy's agent. Most caddies are not like that. Most caddies will go talk with their buddies first and see what they think and maybe not even tell the player at all. In a game where you see a lot of backstabbing, it's really refreshing. The fact that I can trust him is more important than anything."[27]

Not only does Tesori provide Simpson with an extra pair of trustworthy eyes, he also helps check his boss's attitude when necessary — call it a course correction of sorts where Simpson has gotten off track in his thinking. It's in these times, when playing well has nothing to do with drivers and irons and everything to do with the mind and the heart, where Tesori steps in with a simple question.

"How's your joy?" he often asks Simpson.

"Something Paul and I often talk about is our attitude when we go out onto the course," Simpson says. "Are we out here to serve ourselves and seek our own pleasures or are we out here to play for God and His glory."[28]

One of the pair's running themes for the 2011 season was doing their best at all times. The discussion about godly excellence usually brought up one of their favorite Bible stories, David and Goliath.

"Our favorite part of the story is how the Bible says David ran quickly to the battle line," Simpson says. "David believed in His God despite the fact that he was physically outmatched by his opponent. We want to run quickly like David did. We're going to believe in our God. David wasn't wrapped up in whether or not he was going to win. He just believed that his God would never fail him."[29]

Family Matters

As far as Simpson is concerned, there's a direct correlation between integrity and that spirit of David, or attitude of excellence, not just on the golf course but everywhere else in his world. And quite frankly, Simpson's world is usually located in the same general vicinity of his wife, Dowd, and son James (born February 2011).

"Whether I win a golf tournament or I lose a golf tournament, I always try to tell my wife that it doesn't matter," he says. "She's far more important than a tournament win or a disappointing loss."[30]

Simpson's son is too young to understand that concept, but you can believe his dad feels the same way about him. As the elder Simpson has grown more popular with success, he has experienced an increased level of interest within the golf community and is more recognizable in the public eye. While that does bring more pressure, it also brings more opportunity to share an important message.

"One thing I want people to know about me is just how much I care for my wife and my son and how important family is to me," Simpson says. "It's easy to get wrapped up in this golf world and find my identity in being a golfer. But I want everyone to know that I want my identity to be in the fact that Christ and my wife and son mean more to me than golf."[31]

Webb Simpson with his wife Dowd and son James
↓

That's where Simpson's desire to be excellent ties back to integrity. Giving his best to God is actually a display of integrity. This is also true for his wife and son. As discussed in chapter one, husbands are called to love their wives in the same way that, "Christ loved the church" (Ephesians 5:25).

For that reason, Simpson believes that "the most important and sacred relationship that exists on earth is between a husband and a wife."[32] And how can we truly have integrity (or "soundness of moral character")[33] if we don't even have a Christ-like love for our spouse?

"The ways I try to be a great husband usually have to do with my own heart," Simpson admits. "If I'm seeking the Lord at all times, then that allows me to be able to serve my wife in a way that she is worthy to be served. But when I'm falling short in my relationship with God, that's when I start to make mistakes and fail to serve my wife like I've been called to do."[34]

Simpson says his heart is broken when he sees so many marriages that are "either run up dry or falling apart."[35] He's especially troubled by the source of failure: lazy husbands that aren't putting enough love and effort into the relationship.

"I'm so young at it and I'm so new to it, but daily, my goal is to see how I can keep from being a burden on my wife and how I can be a blessing instead," Simpson says. "The only way that I'm ever able to do a great job is when I'm humbling myself before the Lord and humbling myself before my wife."[36]

The same is true for his role as a young father. Even when little James was just a few months old, Simpson says he could see the correlation between he and his wife's relationship and the way he seeks to serve his son. When reading Proverbs 22:6, Simpson is reminded of his responsibility and the positive impact his example and his teaching will have as his boy grows older: "Train

←
The Simpson Family

a child in the way he should go, and when he is old he will not turn from it."

Integrity is a benchmark principle that Simpson hopes to share with his son. He can already point to the way he has handled difficult circumstances, like calling a penalty on himself despite the financial costs, as a future lesson he'll likely share. Finances in general provide a great opportunity for modeling integrity. It's often been said that you can judge a man's heart by the way he spends his money. But in Simpson's case, he wants his son to also gauge his integrity by the limited value he places on material things.

Simpson is reminded of a sermon he once heard in which the pastor told a story about his four-year-old son who wanted a train set for Christmas. Desiring to grant his son's wish, the man bought him a ten-piece set and frustratingly put it together until the wee hours of Christmas Eve. The next morning, his son was predictably excited and screamed for joy. But when the father asked his son if he could play with one of the trains, the boy looked at him and said, "No! It's mine!"

That story really hit home with Simpson who understands how easy it is to claim possessions as his own while failing to realize that everything really belongs to God. In Psalm 50:10, David writes (as a messenger for God) that "every animal of the forest is mine, and the cattle on a thousand hills."

Yet in this age of man-made technology and pervasive do-it-yourself attitudes, Simpson says its no wonder God only requires ten percent of our earnings as part of the Christian tradition often referred to as tithing (see Leviticus 27:30; Malachi 3:10; et al).

"He knows how sinful and selfish our hearts are," he says. "I think tithing is the least we can do to try to be faithful with what God's given us. The way my wife and I like to look at it is it's all God's and we'd better be good managers of what He's given us or He will gladly discipline us."[37]

The Influence of Integrity

How Simpson handles his business is first and foremost a product of his desire to honor his relationship with God. But it also has an impact on family. As the leader of his household, he is called to set the tone by making sound decisions based on biblical principles of integrity. In this regard, he is afforded great influence over them, especially with his son who will look up to him as he grows up and begins to look to his father for instruction and direction.

But the influence of integrity is more far-reaching than that small circle. For some people, it may not be that much bigger, but rest assured, people are watching and the opportunity to have a positive impact is directly tied to reputation. In 1 Peter 3:16, the Apostle reminds the early Christians to have "a good conscience, so that, when you are slandered, those who revile your good behavior in Christ may be put to shame" (ESV).

The reverse of that is also true. The follower of Christ sets himself up for intense scrutiny and disdain when his actions do not match up with his words. And the taller the platform, the harder the fall will be.

"When you're in the public eye and you mess up, everyone's going to find out about it," Simpson says. "Everyone will question anything good you've done up to that point. Even if you've been faithful for 20 years and proclaimed Christ for 20 years, they're going to neglect everything you've ever said."[38]

That doesn't mean we should hide under a rock for fear of failure or bringing dishonor to God's name. As Simpson says, it's true that "the more influence you have, the more careful you need to be."[39] But Christians are ultimately called to use whatever influence we possess to fulfill the charge that Christ gave in Matthew 5:16: "Let your light shine before men, that they may see your good deeds and praise your Father in heaven" (NIV).

That's something Simpson is getting more used to living out every day.

"In the past, I've been too reclusive," he admits. "My wife keeps telling me that God has given me this talent for a reason. I need to glorify Him with it as much as I can and that means having conversations with as many people as I can about why I do what I do. The better I play, the more things come our way."[40]

Sometimes, the things that come his way (and our way, for that matter) aren't good, like wind that moved his ball at the Zurich Classic and effectively blew close to half a million dollars out of his grasp. Ironically, that rule (Rule 18-2b) was modified after the 2011 season. Now the penalty will not apply "when it is known or virtually certain that (the golfer) did not cause the ball to move."[41]

But even if the rule hadn't changed and Simpson faced the exact same circumstance, he would undoubtedly make the same choice. "Looking back, I've seen how God has used that situation to affect other people," Simpson says. "I heard from a lot of people who were watching with their kids and they were able to teach their kids a cool lesson in that moment. It was a small thing I did that wasn't even noble; it was just part of the game. But the Lord definitely used it."[42]

Maybe that's the real purpose behind integrity. Certainly the biblical principle is in place as a means by which the believer can honor God, but as His messengers of the gospel, it's integrity that often sets us apart, allows a trust to be forged, and provides the greatest opportunities to tell others the Good News.

"In a relationship, integrity is important whether it's between 2 people or 150 people," Simpson says. "If integrity is lost, then people begin to question everything. That's why it's so important that we have men and women of integrity today. Without integrity, we lose that chance to change somebody's life."[43]

BACK 9

1	What's your favorite thing about golf?	It is universally the best sport for this reason. My dad and his buddies who are all about 10 handicappers can have a match where coming down the 18th hole, to them, is like they're at the Masters. They're all square and it comes down to whoever makes the putt to win.
2	What's your least favorite thing about golf?	The amount of time I spend away from home.
3	What's your favorite golf course?	Augusta.
4	What's your favorite tournament?	Wells Fargo Championship.
5	What's your favorite hole?	The 13th hole at Augusta.
6	What's the toughest hole you've ever played?	The 12th hole at Sunriver Resort in Oregon (host to the 2006 NCAA Championship).
7	What's your favorite club?	My putter.
8	Who is your favorite playing partner?	Pat Perez. He's hilarious.
9	With what legend in their prime would you most enjoy playing 18 holes?	Ben Hogan.

SCORECARD

Birthdate	August 8, 1985
Birthplace	Raleigh, NC
Residence	Raleigh, NC
College	Wake Forest (2008, Religion)
Nationwide Tour Victories	0
PGA Tour wins	2 (2011 Wyndham Championship, 2011 Deutsche Bank Championship)
Top 25 finishes	36
Top 10 finishes	18
Career PGA Tour money	$8,608,449

*All stats through the 2011 season

How integrity is reflected in our finances.

the

It seems quite appropriate that each hole on a golf course is located on a smooth surface called "the green." After all, big money in the pro game is so often won or lost with the putter.

Just ask Bernhard Langer.

Putting isn't exactly Langer's favorite part of the game. The World Golf Hall of Fame inductee and two-time Masters champion has accomplished great things in spite of bouts with a condition commonly referred to as "the yips" — an uncontrollable twitch in the hands and wrists that causes some afflicted golfers serious trouble with even the simplest tap-ins.

But during the final round of the 2009 Charles Schwab Cup Championship, something equally inexplicable was the source of Langer's angst — a three-foot putt.

"I lined the ball up on the 13th hole and made a practice putt, then put the club down," Langer recalls. "As I looked at the ball, it just moved a smidgen. I mean it moved maybe two millimeters, but I could tell that the black line, where I'd lined it up, wasn't on top of the ball anymore. It had changed slightly to one side. Nobody would have ever noticed so I called the official and told him my ball moved. It was determined that I had addressed the ball, so I got a penalty. It turned out, that one shot cost me $320,000."[1]

Langer talks about the large sum of money very matter-of-factly. It's quite common for one or

money list

"Everything we have is God's. I came into this world with nothing. I'm going to leave this world with nothing. Anything that He entrusts to me—my time, my talent, my treasure, my kids, my wife, my family—is a gift from God. I have to be a good steward of that. I'll be accountable for that when I stand before Him."

— Jonathan Byrd

two strokes on the scorecard to make the difference in making the cut at a tournament (which means getting into the money), placing higher on the leader board (which means getting more of the money), winning the tournament (which means getting a lot more of the money), or even determining a golfer's placement on the money list (which sometimes means keeping or losing a Tour card).

Take for instance the Players Championship, one of the largest purses on the PGA Tour. In 2011, tournament winnings totaled $9.5 million. K.J. Choi defeated David Toms in a playoff to win $1.71 million, while Toms took home a healthy $1.026 million. The one-stroke difference in the playoffs was worth an extra $684,000 for Choi.[2]

Even at the 2011 Reno-Tahoe Open, one of the Tour's smallest purses, a one-stroke victory for Scott Piercy over Pat Perez resulted in a $216,000 prize differential.[3]

But sometimes, the decision to do the right thing and take a penalty stroke can play into a golfer's financial security. PGA Tour regular Kevin Streelman recalls a time when making the wrong decision would have been easy and, at least in the short-term, beneficial to his thinning wallet.

"I was on the mini tours and I was dead broke," he says. "I was playing well in a Gateway Tour event at Wigwam Resort in Phoenix and was tied for the lead heading into the 15th hole. I was playing great, but I hit the ball into the rough. The ball was in this tall Bermuda grass and when I took the club back, the ball just fell back about a quarter of an inch. It was at the point where I couldn't stop myself. I ended up hitting the shot within four feet of the hole and I hit the putt. But then I had to tell everyone that my ball had moved and I had to add a stroke. I ended up losing the tournament by one shot."[4]

At the time, it seemed like a "huge deal"[5] to Streelman. The difference between first and second place was roughly $7,000, and that kind of money would go a long way for a young, struggling golfer. But as time passed, some of the golfers that played in that tournament would bring up Streelman's noble choice and continue to mention it still today. It's an occasional reminder that a man's reputation is much more valuable than whatever might be in his bank account.

For Langer, Streelman, and other Christian golfers, the money issue boils down to having the right perspective. "The greatest lesson we can learn in this life is dependence upon God," Jonathan Byrd says. "I don't think there is any area in life that brings you more to dependence than money when things aren't going well."[6]

It's in those times when we truly come to embrace the scriptural depiction of God as Jehovah Jireh or "The Lord will provide" (Genesis 22:14; NKJV).

All over the Bible we are reminded that God wants to take care of our needs and He will do so if we do two simple yet often difficult things: trust Him and seek Him.

The first part of the equation is encouraged in Proverbs 3:5 where King Solomon writes, "Trust in the Lord with all your heart and lean not on your own understanding."

This is a challenging proposition for anyone going through a financial struggle such as unemployment, insufficient wages, or stacks of bills that might have been incurred due to medical costs or other unforeseen circumstances. But Jesus Himself puts some more weight behind this truth in Matthew 6:25–34 where He encourages the people to "do not worry about your life, what you will eat or drink; or about your body, what you will wear" (verse 25).

Following this exhortation is very counterintuitive to the human spirit. We are always looking for solutions to our problems. Turning to God for our needs tends to be the last thing on our list of things to try during times of trouble. But beyond simply trusting God to provide, we should always couple that action with what Jesus teaches about in verse 33: "But seek first his kingdom and his righteousness, and all these things will be given to you as well."

In other words, put God first and the things that matter to Him first, and everything we worry about, like food, clothes, vehicles, houses, etc., will be provided. It might not be exactly what we want, but it will always be exactly what we need.

That includes enough resource to allow for opportunities to help others. In 1 Timothy 6:18, the Apostle Paul tells his disciple to command those in the church with wealth "to do good, to be rich in good deeds, and to be generous and willing to share."

Stewart Cink takes Paul's admonition to heart. He understands how blessed he is to make a good living by playing the game he loves. "We try to make our financial decisions based on biblical principles," Cink says. "The Bible teaches a lot about money. I think it's one of the topics most dealt with in the Bible. A big part of our financial plan is giving. We feel like the Bible encourages and demands a lot of giving. We've certainly been blessed financially, so we try to honor that."[7]

Cink has experienced another biblical truth found in Luke 6:38 where Jesus says, "Give, and you will receive. Your gift will return to you in full — pressed down, shaken together to make room for more, running over, and poured into your lap. The amount you give will determine the amount you get back" (NLT).

It doesn't really matter who wins or loses any given tournament. Neither does it matter where any given golfer lands on the money list. What does matter to God is what they do with the financial rewards that come from playing a lucrative sport.

The same is true for all who trust in God for their financial, physical, emotional, and spiritual needs. After all, as Webb Simpson says, "It's all God's and we'd better be good managers of what He's given us. He's the one who gave us the ability to acquire it in the first place."[8]

Integrity Has No Secrets.

Stewart

Stewart Cink doesn't remember when he first started playing golf.

"I've been playing before my memory," he says.[1]

Cink chuckles a bit after making that statement, but it's hard to know if he's joking or serious. As the older of two children (he has a younger sister), he does remember his parents taking the family on regular golf outings as soon as he was big enough to sit relatively secure on a cart. Cink has fond memories playing at Florence Country Club in Florence, Alabama.

"My parents weren't really good players but they got to be pretty good," Cink says. "Both my parents eventually got down to single digit handicaps. I just picked it up because they did it. My dad taught me a little bit, but really I learned the values and the enjoyment from my parents and I learned the zeal for it and developed the quest to get better on my own from just playing."[2]

Perhaps neither of his parents turned into a great player, but Cink certainly did — one of the world's best even. Since joining the PGA Tour in 1995, he has won six events including the prestigious Open Championship in 2009. Cink has been a member of five Ryder Cup teams (including the championship team in 2008) and four Presidents Cup teams (all of which won). Cink also ranks just outside the top ten on the PGA career money list with over $30 million in earnings.[3]

Cink

"The number one thing is peace and contentment. In life, there are few things that can give you true peace. Making decisions with integrity is one of those things that can give you true peace."

— Stewart Cink

But that's not why he fell for the game — although even he admits that experiencing that "winning feeling" as an eight-year old and getting his name in the newspaper sped up the process. It was actually a couple years earlier, when Cink wasn't even able to play at the local course yet, that his heart yearned to be closer to the game.

"I would beg my dad to take me to the golf club on Monday when they were closed so I could play," he recalls. "I'd already started falling in love with just being out on the course and I couldn't wait to be old enough to play for real."[4]

Golf Lessons

Through his love of sports, Cink had the opportunity to learn valuable lessons such as teamwork, discipline, and hard work. He spent eight years, in fact, playing soccer, but found quickly that integrity wasn't necessarily inherent to that game's DNA.

"I got away with a few things in soccer," Cink says. "I never called things on myself and I never looked back. If I got away with a slide tackle or something like that and I didn't get called for it, I never looked back and went over to the other team and said, 'Hey, I think you should get a free kick for that.'"[5]

But there was something different about golf. Certainly he learned all the basic rules that don't allow a player to move the ball to a better lie or conveniently toss the ball from behind a tree. It was something much bigger than that.

"Golf teaches you so much about yourself, like who you really are and what you're made of," Cink says. "Not on the PGA Tour, but growing up as a kid, when there's nobody out there watching and you're having the round of your life and you hit that crooked ball off the last tee box and it ends up stymied right behind a tree. It's going to be very tempting to kick it out of there and say, 'I found it!' That's when golf teaches you a lot about yourself and how you per-

form under pressure, when the heat is on. It tells you about how you're going to perform under pressure in other areas of your life."[6]

Cink didn't just learn that from the game, he especially learned it from the people who taught him the game. His first major influence was Chris Burns who was his club pro at Florence Country Club. Although he didn't take lessons from Burns, he did work for him and admired his intense respect for the game.[7]

As a fan of golf, Cink watched players like Jack Nicklaus and Tom Watson. He remembers being drawn to another star golfer, Ben Crenshaw, whom Cink says "was always a guy that was a real gentlemen who showed integrity within the game."

Once Cink joined that elite group of golfers on the PGA Tour in 1995, he was drawn to contemporaries who were several years his senior but whose examples as both professionals and Christians were hard to ignore. Even before he became a believer himself, he understood the integrity and faith exhibited by Bernhard Langer, Tom Lehman, and Larry Mize, among others. Cink remembers one situation in 1998 (just his second full year on the Tour) at the Canon Greater Open in Hartford, Connecticut, where Mize showed incredible grace and class in what would otherwise be deemed a brutal circumstance.

"Larry was cruising to the win," Cink recalls. "Late in the round, he was playing a par four hole that you can drive on, but he played it safe and laid up with an iron. Larry ended up pushing his shot into the trees. He lost his ball and made double bogey on a hole where every once else was making birdies."[8]

Instead of winning the tournament, Mize opened the door for Cink and Olin Browne who ended the round with the same score. Ultimately, Browne won the tournament on the first hole of the playoff, but it was the lesson Cink learned that has lasted longer than any result or money prize could.

"I remember the way he acted in the playoff," Cink says. "He was pleasant. He was encouraging to us. He was living his life that moment just like he lived it before he made double bogey, which I thought was pretty impressive. Larry's always been one of the guys that I've enjoyed playing with out there. He's a calm character and really peaceful. That moment stuck out to me. He'd just given away that tournament and now he was fighting it out with Olin and me in a playoff and still acting really nice and respectful. That had a big impact on me."[9]

Turns out that Cink has likewise had an impact on the golfing community. Jonathan Byrd has always been impressed by Cink's solid Christian walk and a personality that has afforded him the blessing of many good friends on the Tour.

"People like being around him," Byrd says. "He has great enthusiasm. He has a great spirit about him. He's easy to be around. It just seems like the good and the bad roll off his back easily. He doesn't wear his emotions on his sleeve. He has this great joy about him."[10]

Sports psychologist Morris Pickens works with Cink and often hears him use the phrase, "Well, that's not right." It's the golfer's usual response to a situation where he might have the opportunity to partake in a questionable business deal or handle a scenario involving a teacher or sponsor in a way that might be ethical in the world's eyes yet would be deemed self-serving in God's eyes.

"During the 2010 season, Stewart was thinking about changing agents," Pickens says. "They didn't have a written contract but they'd been together for a long time. Stewart was also getting ready to go into his next Nike deal, but he knew the agent had worked on it. If he wanted to, Stewart could've kept that money for himself. Instead, he knew it wasn't right and he figured out what was fair. And for Stewart, what's fair is usually what's overly fair to the other guy and maybe fair to himself. That's just the way he is."[11]

The Perfect Swing

At the time of the playoff in Hartford, Cink was still a new Christian. Perhaps that's why Mize made such an impression on him that day. He knew about the importance of integrity from a secular, competitive point of view, but now he was learning what it looked like to have the peace of mind and confidence that comes with a lifestyle that embraces godly righteousness. And while it hasn't necessarily made him a better golfer, striving for a life of integrity has brought some elements to his game that allow him do his best.

With son Reagan, caddying in Masters Par Three Contest in 2005

↓

With Lisa en route to 2006 Ryder Cup in Ireland

↓

↑

Family on safari in South Africa in 2005.

"For instance, having a disciplined practice schedule helps a lot," Cink says. "If you have a disciplined workout schedule, that helps a lot. It helps if you're disciplined with your diet and you get enough rest and sleep. It's a lot easier to make those decisions if you live with integrity and you're used to making the right decisions. It even gets down to something as minute as keeping an organized calendar for meetings and practice times and staying organized at home. I don't mean keeping every speck of dust out of the shoe drawer. But you need to be organized, and keeping your time organized is made easier by having integrity in your life."[12]

Then there are those things that directly impact the golfer's game and more specifically the golfer's swing. Cink describes his perfect swing this way: "The feel is in the release. The release is when the club head passes the hands. I can only swing the club in a fully released kind of way when I'm at total peace with where the result might end up. If I can swing with a calm and peaceful state of mind and feel that release right at the perfect time without worry, that's my perfect swing."[13]

Cink says he can only perform his best and hit that perfect swing when he's in a "calm and peaceful state of mind."[14] For him, that means being prepared and adhering to the aforementioned schedule of disciplined training, practice, and nutrition.

"I know all the preparation that needs to be in place for me to feel really good," Cink adds. "It may not be that I've hit the right amount of seven irons or sand wedges or putts. It's more about knowing in my mind that I've done what I can do. That enables me to get to the first tee with a confident, bold mindset. It doesn't guarantee success. Just like when you're swinging your driver trying to hit a 300-yard shot down the middle of the fairway, you're never going to do it right every time, but you want to increase the percentage that you'll do it right more often."[15]

Cink takes the same approach in his personal life as he does on the golf course. He prepares for whatever scenarios might come his way in the home as the husband to Lisa or the father to teenage sons Connor and Reagan so that he can make quality decisions with integrity. Cink's spiritual training consists of regular prayer time, consistent devotion in God's Word, and instruction from spiritual mentors.

"The most important thing inside my house is that I provide a good example to my kids, especially when they see me going through adversity," Cink says. "How do I handle that? When the kids look at the father going through difficult times and stress and strain, I think that's when they're watching the closest. For me, I remind myself of that all the time because when life gives you little difficulties, like driving in bad traffic or car problems or running late or a cancelled meeting, when stuff like that happens, that's when the kids really watch. You can teach them

something about dealing with those things with integrity."[16]

Not surprisingly, Cink says it's those times he's struggling at home — specifically in his relationship with his wife — when he has the hardest time staying focused on the golf course.

"There are great benefits to being a professional golfer but that's one of the tough things," Cink admits. "It's really hard to maintain a good relationship with the wife. I've got teenage boys and there are always things happening at home that try our patience. When I can't be there, it stresses both of us out. There are plenty of times when we argue and fight about things. That bothers me. It does. It makes it really hard to be at my best. Being a professional, I have to set it aside and go out and do my best on the golf course. I can always come back and discuss things later on, but it is tough. No matter how well you think you're doing at setting it aside, it's always around and it's easy to go back and think about that stuff if something's bothering you."[17]

But at the end of the day, Cink always comes back to integrity and what that looks like within the context of a family unit. And for him, it's inextricably linked to another key principle that was taught and lived out by Jesus. Cink is reminded of the popular WWJD bracelets that ask the question, "What Would Jesus Do?"

"There are so many things that Jesus would do," he says. "But the number one thing that Jesus would always do is put others first."[18]

Harbour Town Heat

Just like so many other golfers, Cink has faced many tests of integrity within the context of the most common scenarios. Like Webb Simpson, he's dealt with the wind-blown ball on the putting green after addressing the ball and grounding his club. And while playing in a tournament with his alma mater Georgia Tech, he accidentally brushed the bunker sand with his club on the backswing and incurred a two-shot penalty — even though no one else saw what might have seemed like a minor infraction.

But at the 2004 MCI Heritage hosted by the Harbour Town Golf Links in Hilton Head Island, South Carolina, Cink's integrity was tested when doing the right thing played out in his favor. While competing in a playoff, Cink hit his ball into a waste area, sometimes called a waste bunker. These are areas of the course that are "unmaintained or unprepared by grounds crew" and have "a sandy or gravelly surface area."[19] At Hilton Head, most waste areas are composed of crushed shells. From a distance and on television, they often look like a sand bunker, but unlike bunkers or water hazards, waste areas are not considered a hazard and do not require a penalty.

"It was confusing at the time for some of the players that there was a difference between the waste area and the bunkers," Cink recalls. "I was able to move some of those impediments away from my ball. I picked the shells away one at a time until I had a pretty clean lie. There was a rules official with us and I cleared it with him before we even got there. I asked him what I was allowed to do, not because I didn't know, because I already knew. I asked him that so he would know exactly what I knew. I was just making him aware of what I was going to do and that I knew exactly what I could move."[20]

When Cink moved some of the shells away from his ball, many television viewers called in to the tournament believing that he had improperly moved the debris. And even at the end of the playoff, where Cink won with a birdie on a fifth hole, the officials reviewed the video for a lengthy period of time making sure that no infraction had taken place.

"It was stressful even though I knew I'd done nothing wrong," Cink says. "And it was a little embarrassing. The worst part of it was the next day when my competitor in the playoff was vocal and outspoken about his belief that I was wrong and that I should have been disqualified from the playoff or assessed a penalty. He talked with the media and of course the media outlets were calling me and trying to get me to respond. That's where I was tested. I felt an urge to lash out and defend myself, but I also felt like the right thing to do was to stay quiet and let the rules stand behind me and know that I did nothing wrong."[21]

The following week, Cink continued to feel the heat but elected to stand down even though he felt his name was being dragged through the mud. He also approached his former competitor at the next tournament in an effort to explain his position and ultimately clear the air. But that still didn't take away all of the sting and in fact stuck with Cink for the next couple of months.

"Even though I hadn't done anything wrong, I felt like I was a cheater because I was being portrayed that way by a few individuals and it really hurt," he says. "I felt like the win was tainted by events that took place afterward, which was really difficult. It was a testing period. But instead of trying to defend myself, I let the facts speak for themselves and in the end I was totally exonerated. At times I felt like I was a tiny man. Sometimes making a decision in favor of integrity does make you feel a little bit weak. That's human nature."[22]

The Heart Test

Even though Cink struggled with the events surrounding his Harbour Town victory, he never had any regrets about the way he handled the situation, and that certainly is still the case today. That's because there is no guilty conscience associated with doing the right thing. Cink understands the truth found in Proverbs 10:9, which says, "Whoever walks in integrity walks securely, but he who makes his ways crooked will be found out" (ESV).

Of course, back in 2004, Cink might have felt like crying out to God like David did in Psalm 26:1 when he wrote, "Vindicate me, O Lord, for I have walked in my integrity, and I have trusted in the Lord without wavering" (ESV). But the world's perspective rarely matches up with God's, and that fact keeps Cink grounded in a desire to please God first and foremost and let Him take care of the aftermath.

"There are a lot of witnesses out there who can see things, but most importantly God's the one who matters," he says. "You may think you're alone and those are the most tempting times to do something you shouldn't do, but those are also the times when the most important witness is watching you."[23]

That sobering thought keeps Cink on his toes at all times and helps ensure that his head and his heart are always in the right place when big decisions come along or when those snap decisions need to be made throughout the day. Cink refers to it as "the heart test."

"It doesn't take very long," he says. "It doesn't require a whole lot of thinking. If my heart's right with it, then it's fine. Almost never would my heart say, 'Yes, this is the right thing to do' and then would I feel any guilt about it. That's it. But you have to be honest with yourself and be confident in what God's Word says."[24]

When our hearts match up with God's heart, then we are on the road to living the way 2 Peter 3:14 calls us to live, "spotless, blameless and at peace with (God)." And in Psalm 119:1, we read that, "Blessed are those whose ways are blameless, who walk according to the law of the Lord."

On the other hand, when we have guilt tucked away in our heart, not only do we hold back God's blessings, we also keep our lives from moving forward in the direction that He has ordained. "Guilt causes us to underperform," Cink concurs. "It's like a clogged fuel injector on a car. Secrets and guilt work against your integrity in almost every way."

And for the follower of Christ, that's a big problem considering His words in Luke 9:62: "No one who puts his hand to the plow and looks back is fit for service in the kingdom of God." In other words, when we are constantly looking over our shoulder, we become virtually useless to God. Our effectiveness as believers and as functioning human beings is "clogged" up and slowed down.

Sometimes being blameless or guilt free means doing the right thing despite the consequences to others. Cink has been through several instances where friends have been involved in extra-marital affairs. In those situations, he and his wife have been put into the extremely difficult position of handling sensitive information while staying true to their integrity. Whereas Cink has been inclined to take the "that's none of my business" approach, his wife Lisa has challenged him to swiftly confront the issue.

On family hiking
trip in Oregon
Cascades in 2007.

"She wants to keep everything open and honest," Cink says. "And that's really the right way to do it. If you find out something like that about another person in another relationship and you don't say anything, you're carrying the secret just like they are. It starts to wear on you. My wife believes that the best thing to do is to talk about it right away with the person. In situations I've had to deal with, I've used her method and I'm not going to say it fixes everything because not one time has it ended good for the other couple, but at least it keeps me out of the guilt cycle."[25]

Keeping friends accountable can be one of the toughest requirements for living with integrity. Sometimes doing what's right in those situations can actually feel like the exact opposite, especially when the stakes are so high and can have significant ramifications. Perhaps that's what Solomon meant when he wrote, "There is a way that seems right to a man, but in the end it leads to death" (Proverbs 16:25). On the flip side, sometimes God's way seems like the cruel, uncompassionate thing to do. Why not let the sinful activity continue? As long as it's a secret, no one will get hurt, right? According to Numbers 32:23, that secret may not be a secret forever. "You may be sure that your sin will find you out," the writer warns.

In the long term, it really is better for these things to be dealt with sooner than later. It gives the ones involved the chance for redemption and saves the ones being hurt from some of the pain and gets the healing process started. Confronting issues amongst friends doesn't mean blowing up the situation with bluster and bravado. In fact, Jesus tells us to do the exact opposite when instructing how to deal with sin in the Church. Reading Matthew 18:15–17 might be a good starting place for those looking to handle a sensitive situation in a biblical manner.

For Cink, reluctantly getting involved in his friends' problems serves as a reminder of why living with integrity is so important. Seeing other athletes take nasty falls also provide the occasional cautionary tale. Cink was especially shaken by the revelation of Tiger Woods personal struggles and the firestorm that ensued.

"It was really disturbing for me to hear almost the enjoyment the reporters had when they were talking about Tiger's situation," he says. "They still joke around about it. Society loves to bring down winners."[26]

Cink has found that to be even truer for Christians who publicly make mistakes. And because of his outspoken nature on the tour, he takes his responsibility that much more seriously.

"I need to set a good example and live by the words that I say," Cink says. "That's especially true with all the social media. Literally, everybody you talk to is media these days. Everyone has a camera phone that can instantly publish a picture or video of you doing something. A lot of people are especially waiting for someone who is a do-gooder to take a fall. It seems like one of the favorite things to do in our society is see someone who's been a big hero fall. I can't imagine what it would mean to me personally if I made a mistake and had to backpedal or if I had to live with myself because I said one thing but acted another way."[27]

Cink knows what hypocrisy looks like and he doesn't want to fall into that trap that so easily ensnares many of us a Christians. It's easy to talk a good game only to fall through on the important detail of actually living it out consistently. That's where Cink's "heart test" comes back into play. When you know God's Word, are led by His Spirit, and understand the importance of integrity, it will be much easier to stay on that "narrow" road that Jesus compels us to walk in Matthew 7:13–14. The margin for error is small and just like golf courses these days, there's trouble to the left and trouble to the right. But doing our best to live consistently with integrity brings peace, blessing, and true fulfillment.

"So many golfers get so torn up over bogies and mistakes and they get so elated over things that they do," Cink adds. "They ride the rollercoaster and they end up emotionally worn out. I think of golf as something I do, not something I am. It irons out the peaks and the valleys. I'm going to make plenty of birdies and eagles and I'm going to make plenty of bogies and doubles and worse. I'd just better be ready for all of them when they come. I want to be the same no matter what."[28]

A group hug after winning 2009 Open Championship at Turnberry.

BACK 9

1	What's your favorite thing about golf?	The challenge.
2	What's your least favorite thing about golf?	The travel.
3	What's your favorite golf course?	Old Course at St. Andrews.
4	What's your favorite tournament?	The Masters.
5	What's your favorite hole?	The Road Hole (17th Hole, Old Course at St. Andrews).
6	What's the toughest hole you've ever played?	The Road Hole (17th Hole, Old Course at St. Andrews).
7	What's your favorite club?	The putter.
8	Who is your favorite playing partner?	Larry Mize.
9	With what legend in their prime would you most enjoy playing 18 holes?	Bobby Jones.

SCORECARD

Birthdate	May 5, 1973
Birthplace	Huntsville, AL
Residence	Duluth, GA
College	Georgia Tech (1995, Management)
Nationwide Tour Victories	3 (1996 NIKE Ozarks Open, 1996 NIKE Colorado Classic, 1996 NIKE TOUR Champion)
PGA Tour wins	6 (1997 Canon Greater Hartford Open, 2000 MCI Classic, 2004 MCI Heritage, 2004 World Golf Championships-NEC Invitational, 2008 Travelers Championship, 2009 British Open Championship)
Top 25 finishes	196
Top 10 finishes	88
Career PGA Tour money	$30,359,823

*All stats through the 2011 season

A game of integrity.

a gentleman's

They call golf "a gentleman's game." But have you ever wondered why? Ask the average PGA golfer and you'll probably get a response kind of like this one: "In my mind, the definition of a gentleman is someone who holds themselves above the norm, above the average person," D.J. Brigman says. "The game of golf seems to rise above all the other sports. That's why it's called 'a gentleman's game.'"[1]

Brigman is correct in his assessment of what that phrase means today, but according to golf historian Rand Jerris, the common modern interpretation is a deviation from the term's original context. "First of all, it has nothing to do with a gender designation, but a code of conduct," he says. "It has to do with social standards and the principles such as integrity, honesty, and respect for your opponent. That is all very much tied into social structures and the British social class."[2]

Jerris, who has served as the director of the United States Golf Association (USGA) Museum since 2002, says that all classes of people participated in the game during the 15th and 16th centuries in Scotland where golf was played on "the common grounds." The community jointly owned these courses and most anyone had access to them.

"It was only in the 17th century when social clubs began to form around the game and you start to get a separation between the wealthier class from the working class," Jerris says. "But that

Game

"The first thing that comes to mind when I think about golf is integrity. You have to call your own infractions and you have to live with yourself if you don't. That to me has always been the hardest part. If you screw up, you have to try to go to bed that night."

— Kevin Streelman

had nothing to do with the game itself. That was based strictly on the social structure."[3]

As clubs continued to be established throughout the 18th century United Kingdom, they were increasingly affiliated with the upper class. That's where golf historian and educator Gary Wiren says the phrase "a gentleman's game" began to take on a more unsavory meaning. "It meant that you were rich and you could afford to play," he says. "It meant you were educated, had attended a university, and were considered to be a gentleman. At that time, the masses no longer played because the ball was too expensive and it cost to be a member of the club."[4]

In fact, Wiren says a golf ball in that era was equal to a man's working wage for three or four days. He likens it to a 21st century worker who makes $300 a day paying $1200 for one ball. "Obviously that was not something that could be handled by the working class," Wiren adds.[5]

But Jerris believes the implication of the phrase "a gentleman's game" does come with some positive historical application. "There's a particularly strong association between the game and the Scottish military," he says. "A lot of the etiquette of the game and the proper conduct such as respect for your opponent, the silent order of play, a lot of those things actually come out of military tradition. Even the word 'caddie' comes from the word 'cadet,' a military position. In addition to the influence of the British upper class, there is also a lot of overlay of military etiquette and structure onto the social aspects of the game."[6]

Still, Wiren feels like the phrase no longer reflects the diverse nature of today's collection of golfers and golf enthusiasts that has expanded to include men and women, all races of people, and a growing population that reflects many socio-economic classes. As a Master Certified Teacher and the founder of the PGA National Academy of Golf,[7] he makes sure to call the game something else when speaking to his impressionable students.

"It's an antiquated phrase," Wiren says. "I wouldn't call it a gentleman's game at all. I would call it a game of integrity."[8]

And even if the current definition isn't exactly historically accurate, that last comment from Wiren is something that few if any PGA golfers will argue against. "Integrity is what makes golf different from other sports," Jonathan Byrd says. "We have rules officials that drive around, but we don't have people policing us and watching everything we do. That's the beauty of our game. I'm not saying there aren't people who don't take advantage of the rules, but the game is set up to say, 'Hey, you're a gentlemen. You know the rules.'"[9]

Integrity Has No Fear.

Ben

Ben Crane is known to be a slow player. If you don't believe it, just ask him. He'll wholeheartedly agree. In fact, Crane's reputation for deliberate shot analysis and painstaking club selection was the inspiration for a satirical video in which the PGA golfer displayed his trademark dry-witted, self-deprecating humor.

Not everyone has found amusement in Crane's quirky style, and that fact caused him some trouble at the 2005 Booz Allen Classic at Congressional in Pinehurst, North Carolina. During the final round, Crane, by his own admission, was playing "slow."[1] His playing partner, South African Rory Sabbatini, became extremely frustrated and according to one reporter his "fuse snapped" by the time they had reached the 17th hole. Sabbatini hit his second shot into a pond just beyond the green and immediately walked that direction before Crane had played his second shot. After Crane's next swing, Sabbatini chipped his ball onto the green, putted out and then retreated to the 18th tee box while leaving his fellow professional (and traditional decorum) behind.[2]

Sabbatini was visibly annoyed as he forced a brutish handshake and swore all the way to the scoring tent. The fans noticed, the officials noticed, and of course, the media noticed.[3] At the end of the round, ABC Sports reporter Judy Rankin asked Crane about the incident. "What's going on?" she inquired. In that moment, Proverbs 15:1 came to Crane's mind.[4]

Crane

"Golf teaches us that the more that we develop integrity in our lives, the more joy we'll experience in life. We have nothing to be ashamed of. Because if we're operating out of the truth, the truth will set us free."

— Ben Crane

A gentle answer turns away wrath.

Instead of taking an easy swipe at his opponent, who had already been booed and accosted by the spectators, Crane put the blame squarely on himself and refused to make any inflammatory remarks.

"That was a defining moment for me because (playing slow) was something that I needed to work on," Crane says. "I think a lot of people originally thought it was about Rory, but it was much more about me and what I could learn from it from my perspective. I wasn't mad at Rory. I just realized that I needed to start playing faster. I also realized that every time you apply God's word to your life, it works out perfect."[5]

Staring Down the Blind Shots

Even in the middle of that blustery, albeit brief, dustup, Crane was relatively peaceful and calm. He wasn't fearful of Sabbatini's reaction or worried about how his response would be interpreted. Crane simply showed grace and integrity by giving a gentle answer and ultimately turning away Sabbatini's wrath (the two would later exchange apologies over the incident).

That's not to say Crane has never dealt with fear, although not for a lack of integrity but for the occasional lack of confidence in his own ability — something that happens to even the greatest golfers. During one of those anxious stretches in his career, the native Oregonian and resident Texan relied on veteran Tour member and close friend Stewart Cink. Crane played with Cink in the final round of the 2003 BellSouth Classic in Atlanta, a tournament Crane won, but utilized some of Cink's advice from a week earlier in the process.

"I'd really been struggling with fear on the golf course and I confided with him about it," Crane says. "Stewart just gave me a lot of great advice and really helped stir my affection for the Lord and directed me how to pray and how to turn it over (to Him). As God would have it, the very next week after I talked to him about that at the PLAYERS Championship, I got paired with him the last day. He really encouraged me coming down the stretch and I ended up shooting 63. I eagled the last hole to win by four. That was a fond memory."[6]

For some, it might seem ironic that Crane's favorite golf course requires some serious intestinal fortitude. But even the most squeamish players can't help but love playing the historic links at St. Andrews in Fife, Scotland.

"I don't like blind tee shots and St. Andrews has a lot," Crane says. "But walking out onto that course and playing those firm greens, no matter if its rainy or sunny, just teaches you everything you want to know about playing golf. I learned so much during my experience there at the 2010 British Open. When you make the turn and the wind is whipping, those holes are so challenging. You have to play so many different shots just to fight the ball into the wind. It's a fantastic course."[7]

When Crane was four years old, he wasn't too worried about blind tee shots. He was content to fearlessly swing Grandpa Spangler's chipping iron just outside his garage. Crane grew up learning the game from a host of family members, including his grandfather and his parents. He would practice putting indoors with a Nerf golf set or later by utilizing a cup in the floor that his uncle installed to create the feel of an actual green.[8]

The game naturally taught Crane about integrity, but those lessons were fortified and contextualized by the instruction of his pastor and close friend Ron Mehl. His college days at the University of Oregon were also an important part of the spiritual growth process. Crane may have faced some blind shots on the golf course (and would face even tougher ones in the future), but as a young man he was determined to make certain he had reliable mentors and friends to help stare down any blind shots that life away from the game might present.

Ben and his wife host a College Golf Fellowship meeting in their home, Dec. 2011.
→

Ben and wife Heather on the course in Hawaii, Jan. 2012
→

"I started meeting with a couple of guys and we just decided we were going to get together and pray once a week and let it go from there," Crane explains. "Out of that little prayer group of four or five guys, one of those guys came out and caddied for me when I had just turned pro and was playing the mini tours. The two of us held each other accountable while we were traveling on the road. That was one of my biggest steps of faith."[9]

Making Tough Calls

While Crane admits struggling at times with those pesky blind tee shots, he can honestly say that fear has never played a factor when making tough calls out on the course. That's not to say his heart hasn't started beating faster in those moments when he instantly knew that he had made a mistake or that an unpredictable quirk of nature had impacted his ball's lie.

"One of the things in golf that's hard to do is call penalties on yourself when no one else sees," Crane says. "At a tournament in Tampa one year, I was getting ready to walk away from my coin and all of the sudden the ball dropped out of my hand and it landed on my coin and the coin moved. So I had to call an official over and ask him if that was a penalty. Sure enough, it was. That's hard to do, but we're always better off in the end because of it."[10]

But for Crane, making tough decisions that reflect integrity doesn't stop once he exits the clubhouse and heads for the house. In fact, it's in his home where the difficult job of prioritization begins. Over time, Crane has concocted a formula that reflects the four things that he is most passionate about and puts them in the proper order.

"Number one is spending time with God," he says. "That starts with prayer and time in the Word. Right now, it also means memorizing Scripture. The second thing is to spend time with my family and to shepherd and grow with my wife and my kids. The third thing is to steward the gift and the platform that I've been given with golf. I work extremely hard at it by putting in my time, energy, and focus into improving, by doing the drills that I've learned, and by exercising and staying in good shape to not only get better but to prevent injury. And the fourth thing is to love and encourage people outside of my family and to experience fellowship with other people who are walking with the Lord and to encourage those people who aren't."[11]

Crane realizes that a four-point answer to a question about priorities isn't as cut-and-dry as it might sound. There are plenty of challenges to his commitments and responsibilities that can easily disturb the peace and invite a fear of failure in any one of those areas to creep into his mind. Perhaps that's why Crane looks at Job in the Old Testament as the perfect example of someone who fought through incredible moments of fear and doubt in order to stay the course, do the right things, and maintain the remarkable integrity for which he would eventually become so well known.

Ben's Team:
(From back to front, left to right)

Marc Wahl, *therapist*

James Sieckmann, *short game instructor*

Joel Stock, *caddie*

Tommy Limbaugh, *manager*

Troy Van Biezen, *therapist*

Lanny Bassham, *mental coach*

Eric Scofield, *spiritual mentor*

Ben Crane

Greg Rose, *swing instructor / golf coach / advisor*

In the first chapter of Job, Satan appeared to be pleased to find no significant remnant of people following God. With his demonic angels by his side, he then approached the Creator for what turned into a fateful conversation. "Have you considered my servant Job?" the Lord asked. "There is no one on earth like him; he is blameless and upright, a man who fears God and shuns evil" (Job 2:3).

Satan then accused God of protecting Job from harm and opined as to how faithful he would be should those protections be lifted. When God allowed Satan to test Job's integrity, the enemy quickly took action and destroyed everything Job owned and even took the lives of his children. Job, however, remained true to the Lord. This, of course, angered Satan who then went to God and presumed that Job's faith would not survive if such an attack were to include his own physical health. God allowed Satan to put all kinds of sickness and disease upon Job but was not allowed to take his life. And even though he questioned God, cried out daily for mercy, and faced accusations from his so-called friends, Job was still considered "blameless and upright."

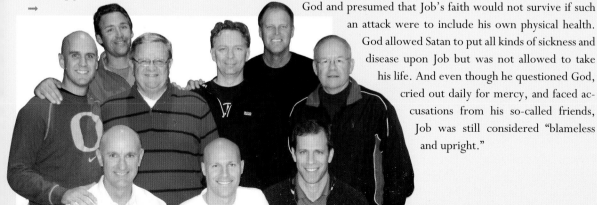

"Even through all of that, Job was so faithful," Crane says. "He lost his family. He lost his health. He lost all of his wealth and absolutely everything, and he still remained faithful. And in the end, God blessed Job with more than he had before because of his integrity, because of his desire to worship God alone, and because he didn't think of the Lord as anything but a good, righteous, and just God."[12]

Job's plight was by no means devoid of serious doubt-filled moments. He most certainly battled fear and frustration, too. "Though I cry, 'I've been wronged!' I get no response; though I call for help, there is no justice," he lamented (Job 19:7). And earlier in the story when Job's wife told him to, "Curse God and die!" (Job 2:9), he surely must have been tempted to end it all right then and there.

But integrity has no fear. It knows that in the end, no matter what troubles come its way, truth will always prevail and God's plan will always be fulfilled "for the good of those who love him, who have been called according to his purpose" (Romans 8:28).

Taking Hard Tests

Crane doesn't claim to have gone through anything remotely close to the trials that Job faced. But just like all of us, he has taken some hard tests in his life. When he thinks about this often difficult journey on the earth, he is reminded of James 1:2–4 and its challenge: "Dear brothers and sisters, when troubles come your way, consider it an opportunity for great joy. For you know that when your faith is tested, your endurance has a chance to grow. So let it grow, for when your endurance is fully developed, you will be perfect and complete, needing nothing" (NLT).

"We really grow in the trials of life," Crane says. "When things are going great, it's easy to become lackadaisical or lazy, but it's in the trials of life where we really find out what our priorities are."[13]

That's why Crane always comes back to those four areas where he has vowed to spend the vast majority of his time — loving God, serving his family, honing his craft, and cultivating meaningful relationships with others. It's also

equally important for Crane to stay alert to the world's devices as the enemy plots to take him off course.

"For me, I've learned that TV is something that just crushes my affections for the Lord," Crane says, for instance. "So one of the biggest things for me is not watching very much TV and not getting engaged in too many sports. Because when I spend too much time with those things, I start to care too much about them and I start to head in the wrong direction."[14]

Crane knows what that's like. When his integrity is in danger of being compromised, he suddenly begins to experience unsettledness and uneasiness in his spirit. His everyday life becomes a struggle and the tough times become nearly unbearable, or as Crane describes it, "an incredibly painful place to be."[15]

"But the benefit of integrity is being able to sleep at night and being able to find rest in your soul," he adds. "Even in the trials of life, when you're operating by God's rulebook, you still experience peace and quiet in it all."[16]

Confidently Facing Fears

Ben & wife Heather
↓

Ben & high school coach
↓

↑

Webb & Ben

Doing the right thing has amazing benefits, but at times can be difficult to follow through. Just like when Crane took some verbal heat from Sabbatini at the Booz Allen Classic or the time he dropped his ball onto his coin marker, there is often a sick feeling in the pit of our stomachs reminding us of the impending choices we are required to make.

For Crane, it always comes back to a quiet confidence he has in knowing that the outcome is infinitely better when integrity rules the day. One of his favorite Scriptures is found in Joshua 1:7–8: "Be strong and very courageous. Be careful to obey all the law my servant Moses gave you; do not turn from it to the right or to the left, that you may be successful wherever you go. Do not let this Book of the Law depart from your mouth; meditate on it day and night, so that you may be careful to do everything written in it. Then you will be prosperous and successful."

In this passage, God is commissioning Joshua to take the leadership reigns from Moses who had just died. It's hard to imagine the Creator of the universe speaking directly to us, but that's exactly what Joshua experienced in that moment. And since the truth of God's Word transcends all generations (1 Peter 1:25), we can boldly embrace this commission as our own. While obeying God's law in of itself won't bring salvation — only a surrendered relationship with Jesus Christ can do that — we can obtain access to many blessings and protections that come from the life of integrity. And just as we saw with Job, this doesn't mean we won't face tough times, but we can confidently and courageously believe that there is a purpose behind it all and that ultimately — whether here on earth or in heaven — we will experience the abundant life that Jesus talks about in John 10:10 (NKJV).

In those times when even the smallest hint of fear and doubt comes our way, we can be remind-

→

Ben, his cousins, and Grandpa Spangler.

→

Ben's first official golf photo

ed of the words Paul wrote his young disciple Timothy: "For God has not given us a spirit of fear, but of power and of love and of a sound mind" (2 Timothy 1:7; NKJV). That's the truth that Ben Crane relies on daily. He also understands that striving to live with integrity is simply "what God calls us to do"[17] and is part of a process that will take us to an incredible destination.

"At the end of the day, if we don't have our integrity, then we're not walking in a right relationship and we're not letting God prune us," Crane says. "If we're allowing God to prune us and make us more like Him, then we're on the greatest journey in this life. That's where we experience true joy, peace, and contentment, and the filling of our cup."[18]

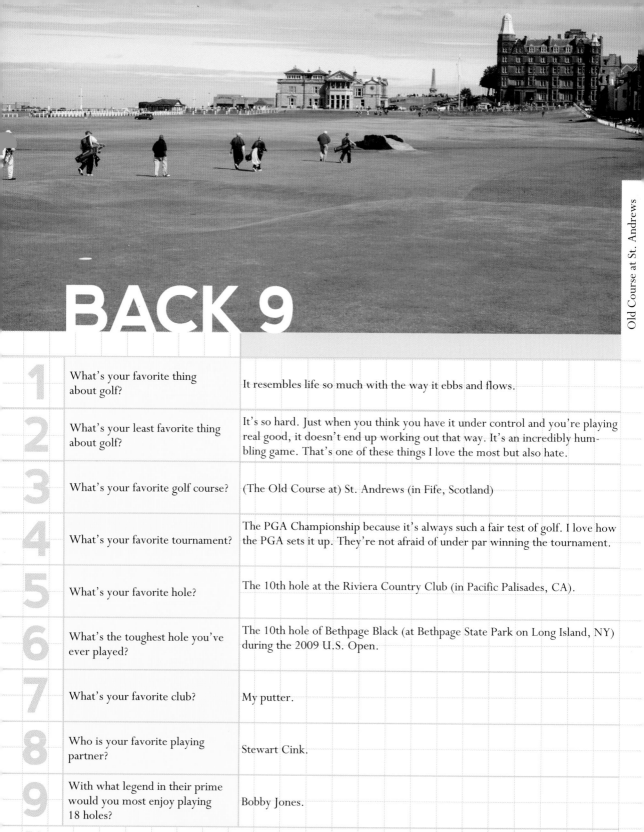

Old Course at St. Andrews

BACK 9

1	What's your favorite thing about golf?	It resembles life so much with the way it ebbs and flows.
2	What's your least favorite thing about golf?	It's so hard. Just when you think you have it under control and you're playing real good, it doesn't end up working out that way. It's an incredibly humbling game. That's one of these things I love the most but also hate.
3	What's your favorite golf course?	(The Old Course at) St. Andrews (in Fife, Scotland)
4	What's your favorite tournament?	The PGA Championship because it's always such a fair test of golf. I love how the PGA sets it up. They're not afraid of under par winning the tournament.
5	What's your favorite hole?	The 10th hole at the Riviera Country Club (in Pacific Palisades, CA).
6	What's the toughest hole you've ever played?	The 10th hole of Bethpage Black (at Bethpage State Park on Long Island, NY) during the 2009 U.S. Open.
7	What's your favorite club?	My putter.
8	Who is your favorite playing partner?	Stewart Cink.
9	With what legend in their prime would you most enjoy playing 18 holes?	Bobby Jones.

SCORECARD

Birthdate	March 6, 1976
Birthplace	Portland, OR
Residence	Westlake, TX
College	University of Oregon (1999, Sociology)
Nationwide Tour Victories	2 (2000 BUY.com Wichita Open, 2001 Gila River Classic at Wild Horse Pass Development)
PGA Tour wins	4 (2003 BellSouth Classic, 2005 U.S. Bank Championship in Milwaukee, 2010 Farmers Insurance Open, 2011 The McGladrey Classic)
Top 25 finishes	31
Top 10 finishes	36
Career PGA Tour money	$15,278,462

All stats through the 2011 season

PROFILES OF INTEGRITY

We've already heard from four of the PGA Tour's biggest names. We've also received insight into various elements of the game and how they impact this enormously important concept of integrity. This book has also featured some commentary from other professional golfers such as the legendary World Golf Hall of Fame member Bernhard Langer, multi-tournament winner Aaron Baddeley, and rising star Kevin Streelman.

In this section, we learn more about these extraordinary men and others like them, including Justin Leonard and D.J Brigman, who have shown a unique ability to skillfully maneuver the world's toughest golf courses while deftly walking out their Christian faith through displays of integrity and servant leadership.

Shinnecock Hills

BACK 9 Justin Leonard

1	What's your favorite thing about golf?	It can never be perfected.
2	What's your least favorite thing about golf?	It takes too long to play.
3	What's your favorite golf course?	Shinnecock Hills (in Southampton, NY).
4	What's your favorite tournament?	The Open Championship.
5	What's your favorite hole?	The Postage Stamp at Royal Troon (in South Ayrshire, Scotland).
6	What's the toughest hole you've ever played?	The 18th at Carnoustie (in Angus, Scotland).
7	What's your favorite club?	My TaylorMade R11s driver.
8	Who is your favorite playing partner?	My dad.
9	With what legend in their prime would you most enjoy playing 18 holes?	Byron Nelson.

Justin Leonard has experienced some of professional golf's highest highs. The Dallas, Texas, native has won 12 PGA Tour events, including the prestigious British Open Championship in 1997 and THE PLAYERS Championship in 1998. Leonard has appeared on five Presidents Cup teams and three Ryder Cup squads that combined for five U.S. victories.[1]

But just like most golfers, Leonard has also spent significant time trudging along in some pretty deep valleys for an athlete of his caliber. Heading into the 2012 season, he hadn't won a tournament since the 2008 Stanford St. Jude Championship and in 2011 he only made the cut in 14 of the 26 events he played.[2]

Through all of those scenarios, Leonard has learned to trust in God, win or lose.

"(My faith in God) changes my golf in that I know that when I'm going through a valley, there is a reason I'm there," he says. "It's shaping my character and making me stronger. Although it's hard to do, I thank God for those times."[3]

Leonard gives much of the credit for his spiritual growth to his wife, Amanda, and PGA Tour chaplains Larry Moody and Dave Krueger. He admits that early in his career he was "very wrapped up" in himself and his game. But after attending his first Bible study at Hilton Head in 2002, "everything started to click."[4]

"(Larry) asked if I had accepted Christ into my life and turned my life over to Him, and I said no I hadn't, but I would like to," Leonard says. "That was kind of the beginning of my journey. And thanks to help from people like Larry and my wife, Amanda, and my Christian brothers out here on Tour, I'm trying the best I can to walk the walk."[5]

Ben Crane is one of the men whose commitment to accountability has encouraged Leonard to spend more time reading the Bible and live with the same kind of integrity away from the game as he does on the golf course.

"Getting in the Word every day is difficult," Leonard says. "But it's that time that I need to focus on God and just for me personally to discover all of the reasons we're here and become closer to Him."[6]

SCORECARD

Birthdate	June 15, 1972
Birthplace	Dallas, TX
Residence	Dallas, TX
College	University of Texas (1994, Business)
Nationwide Tour Victories	Never Played
PGA Tour wins	12 (1996 Buick Open, 1997 Kemper Open, 1997 British Open Championship, 1998 THE PLAYERS Championship, 2000 Westin Texas Open at LaCantera, 2001 Texas Open at LaCantera, 2002 WORLDCOM CLASSIC-The Heritage of Golf, 2003 The Honda Classic, 2005 Bob Hope Chrysler Classic, 2005 FedEx St. Jude Classic, 2007 Valero Texas Open, 2008 Stanford St. Jude Championship)
Top 25 finishes	209
Top 10 finishes	94
Career PGA Tour money	$30,553,771

All stats through the 2011 season

BACK 9 Aaron Baddeley

1	What's your favorite thing about golf?	It's my responsibility to improve and to perform.
2	What's your least favorite thing about golf?	Traveling without my family.
3	What's your favorite golf course?	There are three I really like: Augusta, Carnoustie (in Angus, Scotland), and Kingston Heath (in Melbourne).
4	What's your favorite tournament?	The Masters and the British Open.
5	What's your favorite hole?	The 18th Hole of any British Open.
6	What's the toughest hole you've ever played?	The 18th Hole at Carnoustie.
7	What's your favorite club?	My driver.
8	Who is your favorite playing partner?	There are too many great guys to pick from.
9	With what legend in their prime would you most enjoy playing 18 holes?	Ben Hogan.

On the morning of April 16, 2006, Aaron Baddeley had a lot on his mind. He was celebrating his first-year anniversary with wife, Richelle, and was preparing to share a special Easter Sunday message during a sunrise service at the Harbour Town Golf Links in Hilton Head, South Carolina. Baddeley also just happened to be tied for the lead with Jim Furyk heading into the final round of the Verizon Heritage.[1]

Up until then, Baddeley had yet to win on the PGA Tour. He had won back-to-back Australian Opens (1999 and 2000) and the 2001 Greg Norman Holden Invitational (also held in Australia), but showed little sign of nerves or apprehension. And he certainly had no intentions of pulling out of his commitment to speak to the hundreds of people gathering for the outdoor chapel event. Baddeley was serious about winning the tournament, but he wasn't stressed out either.

"I know that everything is in God's time," Baddeley says. "You've got the promises of the Word that all things work for the good. When things don't go your way you can be like, 'Alright, there's something going on here. Lord, show me what you're trying to teach me.' The promises in the Word are what give you so much peace."[2]

Baddeley went on to shoot one under par that day, which was good enough to defeat Furyk by one stroke. He picked up his second PGA Tour win in 2007 at the FBR Open and ended a four-year drought by winning the 2011 Northern Trust Open.[3]

The attitude he displayed heading into the final round of the Verizon Heritage was a far cry from six years earlier when Baddeley says he almost gave up on the game completely. After winning his first Australian Open, he found himself in a major rut just ten months later and "was playing terrible."

"I really got away from what I enjoyed doing and how much I loved playing the game," Baddeley says. "Then I got back to my goals and started focusing on what I wanted to achieve. Two months later I won the Australian Open again."[4]

Baddeley was born in New Hampshire where his Australian-born father Ron was the chief mechanic for Mario Andretti. The family moved back to Melbourne when he was two years old. Because of that unusual circumstance, Baddeley holds dual citizenship and now resides in Scottsdale, Arizona. He credits both of his grandmothers for teaching him the game of golf at the age of eight and fondly remembers his first trip to the course with grandmother Jean Baddeley.

"I remember my first round with my grandmother's clubs," Baddeley says. "I shot 58 on nine holes and I've never shot higher since."[5]

While he didn't learn golf from his parents, he does credit them for teaching him about integrity. Baddeley accepted Christ at the age of 12 at a youth outreach event where a famous Australian Rules football player was speaking, and his desire to please his parents by being honest and obedient continued to grow. But he admits that for a time he was just going through the motions in his relationship with God.[6]

Then in 2002, Baddeley, at the age of 21, felt that God was calling him to give up dating for a season. So for the next six months, he didn't date or pursue any serious relationships with the opposite sex. "I did it without even thinking," Baddeley recalls. "That was the point where God really got a hold of me. That's where I really started to press in and seek him."[7]

At the same time, Baddeley was making his second attempt to play on the PGA Tour. His first attempt in 2000 was a miserable failure, but now he felt invigorated and ready to take on any challenge — even if that meant

playing on the Nationwide Tour for a time until he was able to work his way back up to golf's top series.

"It wasn't where I wanted to be, but that turned out to be the best year of my life," Baddeley says. "Having a strong relationship with the Lord allowed me to have peace and happiness and joy. The difference was obvious and my friends started to notice a change."[8]

Since Baddeley's breakthrough victory in Hilton Head, fellow Christian golfers on the Tour have picked up on the soft-spoken but affable Aussie's authentic walk with God.

"Aaron Baddeley approaches the game with a great work ethic," Jonathan Byrd says. "He loves studying his Bible. He's got a really good reputation on Tour with a lot of people. He's kind of one of those quiet guys who goes about his work and does his thing and has a lot of success. I don't know anyone who has anything against him for any reason."[9]

His nickname, ironically, is Badds — a moniker given to him by some friends growing up. "It's sort of catchy," he admits. "But my life is all about following the Lord and doing what's right."[10]

And in an age where integrity seems like a lost cause, Baddeley insists that it does matter, if for any reason, because it reflects God's character. "That's what He is all about," he says. "God wants and desires us to live a life as Jesus did and to exhibit His character traits. When we live life with integrity, we show the world God's character through us."[11]

Even though some might not put the two together, Baddeley believes that integrity is directly connected to Christ's command in Mark 12:31 to, "Love your neighbor as yourself," and His instruction in Matthew 7:12 to "do to others what you would have them do to you."

"That's been on the forefront of my heart and mind," he explains. "So each day, I try to treat my wife, friends, co-workers, and family just like I would want them to treat me. Doing what God calls me to do — to be honest, loving, and faithful — that's all part of having integrity."[12]

And whether Baddeley is speaking to a group of people in a church or on a golf course, or simply walking the links with whatever playing partner he has been assigned that day, the life of biblical integrity boils down to one powerful piece of advice.

"Live what you preach," Baddeley says. "As a Christian, you're always going to be under a microscope. You really have to be careful. You've got to live upright and holy. That's the biggest witnessing tool. It's just what James says (in James 2:17). Faith without works is dead. You've got to live out your faith."[13]

SCORECARD

Birthdate	March 17, 1981
Birthplace	Lebanon, NH
Residence	Scottsdale, AZ
College	Lived in Australia
Nationwide Tour Victories	0
PGA Tour wins	PGA Tour wins: 3 (2006 Verizon Heritage, 2007 FBR Open, 2011 Northern Trust Open)
Top 25 finishes	64
Top 10 finishes	30
Career PGA Tour money	$14,098,458

*All stats through the 2011 season

BACK 9 Kevin Streelman

1	What's your favorite thing about golf?	The competition, the camaraderie, being with family, and being outdoors.
2	What's your least favorite thing about golf?	Misbehaving golf balls.
3	What's your favorite golf course?	Chicago Golf Club.
4	What's your favorite tournament?	The Masters.
5	What's your favorite hole?	The 13th Hole, Upper Course, Whisper Rock (Scottsdale, AZ)
6	What's the toughest hole you've ever played?	The 18th hole at the Congressional Country Club (where the 2011 U.S. Open was played in Bethesda, MD)
7	What's your favorite club?	The driver.
8	Who is your favorite playing partner?	Webb Simpson, Rich Beem, and Matt Jones.
9	With what legend in their prime would you most enjoy playing 18 holes?	Bobby Jones.

Not many people in the golfing community will forget the off season leading into the 2010 PGA Tour season. It was during that time when revelations of Tiger Woods' extra-marital affairs became public and were made into worldwide headlines. As Woods suffered through the embarrassment of his actions and a subsequent divorce, everyone else was left in the wake of the inopportune fall of the world's greatest golfer.

That's when Kevin Streelman got the inspiration to do something positive to help offset the negative attention his sport was receiving, and the idea for FCA GAMEDAY was "planted" in his head. Instead of standing by and watching the PGA Tour take a beating, he decided it was the perfect time to be more proactive in reaching out to the game's younger fans. "The last thing Jesus said to the disciples was to go spread the Word to all nations," Streelman says. "If we're not using the platform we've been given to do something to help others, then we're not taking advantage of the gifts he's given us."[1]

Streelman's concept was to allow kids to spend some quality time with a few golfers during nine holes of a Tuesday or Wednesday practice round at a PGA event. The first FCA GAMEDAY took place in 2010 and was expanded to include the majority of the tournaments in 2011. Working with Tour Life director Ben Bost, Streelman, Webb Simpson, Ben Crane, D.J. Brigman, and several other golfers got on board to also include a time of interaction between the kids and the golfers for a Q&A session, photos, and autographs.

"I love seeing these kids' eyes when we speak to them," Streelman says. "They're so intrigued and they're so into the golf and what we're talking about, but more importantly the message we're trying to get across to them. To see their passion and to see their minds start turning is what it's all about for us. That makes it all worth it."[2]

Working with kids has opened Streelman's eyes to the significant influence he and other professional golfers have on young people. He admits that a few years earlier, he wasn't ready for the scrutiny that being a role model invites. But now that he has made a deeper commitment to his faith in God, he actually embraces the challenging responsibility.

"We're watched quite a bit on the golf course," Streelman says. "When kids are out there and they see us speaking at a Search Ministries breakfast or at an FCA GAMEDAY, we hope they're not hearing us speak

but that they're hearing the Lord speak and He's just using us as His microphones to change people's lives. That's what we're ultimately called to do."[3]

Streelman has also found that the more successful he becomes, the bigger his platform grows. And his influence goes well beyond the youth audience and into the world that includes business leaders and fellow golfers with whom he rubs shoulders almost on a daily basis. Streelman is reminded daily of how his witness and example can impact the lives of others, sometimes without even directly saying a word.

"On the PGA Tour, we are in situations where microphones are put on you all the time. If you get angry with a volunteer, an official, or a caddie, people pick up on that. If you're not careful, you can set a bad example for the people you need to be setting the best example for. Sometimes that's the hardest part. The better you do, the more closely

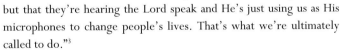

← Kevin Streelman's high school freshman year in Wheaton, IL in 1994

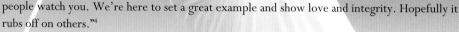

Kevin with wife Courtney, and their dog Snoop; at Duke after winning the UNC Intercollegiate Championship; his junior year at Wheaton Warrenville South High School ↓

people watch you. We're here to set a great example and show love and integrity. Hopefully it rubs off on others."[4]

When Streelman feels like he's sinking too deeply into the privileged lifestyle of the professional athlete, it only takes a quick reflection into his not-so-distant past when he was growing up in Wheaton, Illinois, and traveled across the Chicago area with his family, playing the city's spectacular public golf course circuit. That impressionable time in his life sparked a passion for the game and set his future in motion.

"I still view myself as a cart kid who worked to make a couple of bucks cleaning carts and scrubbing clubs at the local clubhouse," Streelman says. "Now that I'm established on the Tour, I'm slowly getting more recognized at places like the airport. Some people struggle with that. Other people are great at that. You just have to work at it and set the best example you can."[5]

That's where Streelman says good friends and great mentors have played a big part in his life. He and Webb Simpson have become close friends since Simpson's rookie year in 2009. Streelman also looks up to veteran professional Ben Crane whom he describes as "a rock" and "an inspiration." Other key figures in his life have been chaplains Larry Moody and Dave Kruger who work with Search Ministries and provide both verbal instruction and non-verbal modeling of the Christian walk.[6]

Golf has helped teach Streelman plenty of lessons about integrity, but through meaningful relationships and a growing understanding of God's Word, he is truly starting to understand the purpose behind biblically inspired integrity.

"I'm trying to place Christ at the forefront of my life and I'm working on my integrity every single day," Streelman says. "As I've done that, golf has become less and less important to me, but the flipside of that is I've had more and more success. It's funny how that works. It's a challenge. It's a constant battle. It's one of the harder things on this earth because there are a lot of media outlets and a lot of worldly outlets that are trying to tell you otherwise. We're going to fail. We're going to battle. We're going to say things we shouldn't say. It's a constant battle of trying to get better so we can be effective witnesses of what Jesus has done in our lives."[77]

SCORECARD

Birthdate	November 4, 1978
Birthplace	Winfield, IL
Residence	Scottsdale, AZ
College	Duke University (2001, Sociology)
Nationwide Tour Victories	0
PGA Tour wins	0
Top 25 finishes	30
Top 10 finishes	15
Career PGA Tour money	$5,154,198

*All stats through the 2011 season

BACK 9 D.J. Brigman

1	What's your favorite thing about golf?	The view from my office.
2	What's your least favorite thing about golf?	Traveling.
3	What's your favorite golf course?	Olympic Club in San Francisco.
4	What's your favorite tournament?	The Mayakoba Golf Classic in Playa del Carmen, Mexico.
5	What's your favorite hole?	The 18th hole at Pebble Beach.
6	What's the toughest hole you've ever played?	The 18th hole at Doral (in Miami, FL).
7	What's your favorite club?	My putter.
8	Who is your favorite playing partner?	Zach Johnson.
9	With what legend in their prime would you most enjoy playing 18 holes?	Ben Hogan

During the 1993–94 school year in Bedford, Texas, a fair amount of the typical teenage shenanigans were taking place. Girls were trying to score popularity points by dating football players. Guys were chasing after the cheerleaders. And many of them were searching out good times every weekend by drinking and pursuing those aforementioned relationships.

But D.J. Brigman knew something wasn't right. There was a burning desire inside the high school junior to be different. At the time he didn't fully understand why, but later came to realize it was God setting him apart from the stereotypical crowd.

"I wanted to live with integrity and live above what everybody else was doing," Brigman says. "That's when I started to put all my energy into golf and pursuing that as an avenue of going to college and doing something that I really wanted to do."[1]

Brigman's initial test came soon thereafter. Playing in a tournament that same year, he found himself in contention for the first time in his young career. Brigman was battling back and forth with the top-ranked player from a rival high school. Adding to the drama, the two young golfers were in the same group.

Late in the round, Brigman hit his ball into some low-hanging trees. He went into the shaded area to chip it out and noticed a large amount of leaves on the ground. Brigman sat his bag down, went to hit his shot, and just as he addressed the ball it moved. Hidden in the trees, Brigman admits his first thought wasn't the purest.

DJ with son Pierce
(left) and daughters
Delaney (middle)
and Sasha (right)

Well, no one saw it move.

"A few moments later, I knew it wasn't the right thing to do," Brigman recounts. "So I ended up placing it back in the original spot and hit it. When I got to the green, I ended up making a double bogey. The other golfer assumed I'd shot a six, but when I told him what happened, he was shocked that I would call the penalty on myself."[2]

Since then, Brigman says he has faced the same decision many times and he has always made what he felt was the right choice even if it is potentially might cost him a tournament victory or a chance to earn more money.

"Doing what's right is more important than my score or my place on the leaderboard," he says. "That's where I hold myself accountable."[3]

Brigman admits he's not perfect, but in striving to live with integrity he has reaped many benefits in both his personal and professional worlds. On the course, Brigman has sustained a modest ten-year career in both the Nationwide Tour where he has two career victories, and the PGA Tour where he is yet to win a tournament through the 2011 season, but has earned roughly $1.1 million and collected nine Top 25 finishes.[4]

But Brigman has experienced the greatest rewards of integrity in his most important jobs as a husband and father of three children. "I want to be able to look myself in the mirror, holding my chin up regardless of what trials I may be going through in my life or what victories I might be celebrating," he says.[5]

That hasn't always been easy. Brigman admits that he's "tested on a daily basis."[6] Most of those tests have had nothing to do with grounding his club or addressing the ball, but rather come from his experiences as a father. Brigman wants to raise his children by showing them examples of what integrity looks like. Simple things like picking trash up from the ground and throwing it away have given him the opportunity to teach simple lessons about responsibility and doing the right thing.

DJ Brigman as a toddler, pre-teen, and on the golf course.
↓

"Or it might be seeing someone holding up a sign on a street corner and giving them a couple of dollars or giving them a bag with some water and some snacks," Brigman adds. "It might be going through a drive-thru and paying for somebody's meal behind me. Those aren't things you can just talk to them about. You have to show them through daily situations. That's the best way for them to learn. I hope I'm showing them the right things. Time will tell."[7]

Brigman says the life of integrity also brings him peace no matter what is going on around him. Otherwise, he would constantly be riding an emotional rollercoaster with tall climbs, steep dives, and countless loopty-loops.

"That peace affects your health and your stress levels," he says. "If you're doing the right things, regardless of whether it looks like the right things or not, you can live with your decisions and have some peace, even if things don't turn out the way you want them to."[8]

But it's not something Brigman would ever try on his own. He is acutely aware of his need for a relationship with Christ. Without that, his quest for integrity would be empty if not fleeting. Brigman knows he would start to look to fill that void in the same way his high school friends did back in Bedford, Texas.

Perhaps that's why Brigman enjoys speaking to young people so much. He has embraced the opportunity to share his testimony with teenagers and kids through various outreach ministries including the GAMEDAY activities held at various golf tournaments and sponsored by Fellowship of Christian Athletes. When he talks to them from a stage or in one-on-one conversations, integrity is a topic he brings up often.

"Integrity matters because I don't want to be the average person," Brigman shares. "I want to rise above what the average person might do or what the media says we should do. I want to hold myself to a higher standard. Being a Christian is all about rising above and being different, but doing it in a positive way so that people want to know what your faith is all about."[9]

SCORECARD

Birthdate	May 3, 1976
Birthplace	Clovis, NM
Residence	Albuquerque, NM
College	University of New Mexico (1999, Human Resources)
Nationwide Tour Victories	2 (2003 Permian Basin Charity Golf Classic, 2010 Nationwide Children's Hospital Invitational)
PGA Tour wins	0
Top 25 finishes	9
Top 10 finishes	0
Career PGA Tour money	$1,111,489

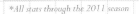

All stats through the 2011 season

BACK 9 Bernhard Langer

1	What's your favorite thing about golf?	First of all, it's being outside in the fresh air and in nature and then it's the different challenge it brings every day.
2	What's your least favorite thing about golf?	Putting.
3	What's your favorite golf course?	Cypress Point (in Monterrey, CA).
4	What's your favorite tournament?	The Masters.
5	What's your favorite hole?	There are so many good ones. If I had to pick one, I'd say the 13th at Augusta.
6	What's the toughest hole you've ever played?	There are a lot of tough ones, too. The 16th at Cypress Point.
7	What's your favorite club?	I don't have one.
8	Who is your favorite playing partner?	I don't have a favorite.
9	With what legend in their prime would you most enjoy playing 18 holes?	Ben Hogan.

Growing up in Anhausen, Germany, Bernhard Langer distinctly remembers a lesson he was taught again and again by his parents. "It was pounded into me that I had to be honest and trustworthy and that people could rely on me," he says.[1]

Amazingly, it was a lesson he almost didn't learn at all.

When Langer's father Erwin was still a young single adult, he was drafted into the German army during World War II. For two years he was a motorbike messenger, but was captured by the Allies and became a P.O.W. While likely headed to Siberia, the train transporting the prisoners stopped at the Russian/German border and several of them (including Langer's father) escaped. He managed to avoid being shot by the Allied soldiers and spent the next few weeks walking westward through the woods at night and hiding during the day. When the war ended, he settled down in Bavaria and married Langer's mother Walburga.[2]

Had his father been shipped to Siberia or, worse, died in his attempt to escape recapture, Langer wouldn't be here today. Instead, he grew up an hour from Munich as the youngest of three children where his father (who passed away in 2006) was a bricklayer and his mother was a housewife. Like many Germans in that day, the Langer family was deeply rooted in the Roman Catholic faith. Langer himself served as an altar boy for ten years.

He also caddied at a young age — 9 years old to be exact — and did so until he was 15. When Langer picked up the game he was a natural and started working as an assistant pro in Munich and advanced to the European tour by the age of 18. He's been a professional golfer ever since.

When the world rankings started in 1985, Langer was considered one of the game's greatest players and was ranked #1 throughout most of 1985 and 1986. His first PGA Tour victory was also his first major championship. At the 1985 Masters, Langer erased a four-shot deficit going into the final round and won the prestigious event by two strokes over Seve Ballesteros, Raymond Floyd, and Curtis Strange.

But the celebration didn't last long. In his first moments of silent contemplation the following day, Langer asked himself a troubling question. Is this all there is?

"I got up and was obviously thrilled with my win and being ranked number one in the world," Langer recalls. "I had just been married for one year. I had a beautiful young wife and lots of material things — houses, cars, basically everything that I could dream of and more. Yet there was still this void inside of me and I couldn't

Bernhard Langer, 18, at the Meunchener Golf Club in 1975.

Langer, 2004 European Team captain, with the Ryder Cup trophy.

pinpoint what it was. I knew there was more, but I didn't know what."[3]

Three days later, the 28 year old attended his first Bible study along with his wife, Vikki. Longtime tour chaplain Larry Moody was sharing the story of Nicodemus found in the third chapter of John.

"He talked about when Jesus said you have to be born again," Langer says. "That's exactly what I needed to hear because I'd heard everything else in church. I could've quoted certain Bible verses. I knew most of the Bible stories. I was never told that before. I was told I had to be a good person and earn my way to heaven and that's clearly not what the Bible says."[4]

That meeting sparked something inside of Langer. He got out his seldom-read Bible and started attending the study group on a regular basis. Langer continued to ask deeper questions and eventually realized what he needed to do next. "It became very clear to me that I had to be born again to have eternal life," he says.[5]

The picture was complete. Langer had always understood the basic need for good moral character and he had always understood how the rules of golf serve as a reminder of what integrity looks like on the course. But now integrity had a greater purpose.

"I've always wanted integrity," Langer says. "I've always wanted to be trustworthy and honest. I grew up that way. But when I accepted Christ and became a believer, then I wanted to be a role model for others and for my kids. Integrity became even more important."[6]

Over his long and storied career, Langer has become known as one of the rock-solid representations of godly integrity throughout the PGA Tour and more recently the Champions Tour. He has been blessed with an enormous platform thanks to a pair of Masters win (Langer also won in 1993), a Ryder Cup victory in 2004 as the European team captain, and two Champions Tour majors (2010 Open Championship and 2010 Senior Open).[7]

And to those who look at him as a credible example of integrity, the wise German golfer's advice remains as simple and understated as you might expect from the soft-spoken World Golf Hall of Fame member. "I don't think there are any bad decisions when you tell the truth and integrity is involved," Langer says. "There's only the truth, and if you tell the truth, that's always the best way to go, even though it might hurt in the short term. In the long term, it's always better. We make decisions every day and some are harder than others. Many of them are very difficult decisions. But I should never compromise my integrity with the decisions I make."[8]

SCORECARD

Birthdate	August 27, 1957
Birthplace	Anhausen, Germany
Residence	Boca Raton, FL
European Tour Wins	42
Champions Tour Wins	14
PGA Tour wins	3 (1985 Masters, 1985 Sea Pines Heritage, 1993 Masters)
Top 25 finishes	119
Top 10 finishes	62
Career PGA Tour money	$10,111,921

All stats through the 2011 season

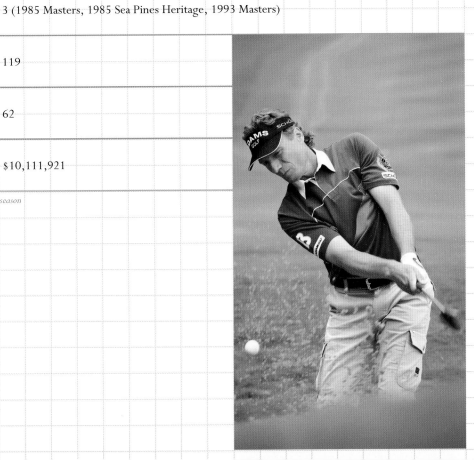

What God Wants to Teach Us about Integrity.

making

There is something uniquely symbolic about tapping in a putt on the ninth green, retrieving the ball and then walking a few yards to the 10th tee box. It's routinely referred to as "making the turn" and, from a practical standpoint, it simply means the golfer has played half the round and is now heading back toward the general direction of the clubhouse where the 18th and final hole awaits.

But sometimes that literal u-turn can present an opportunity for a golfer who might have been struggling up until that point. Or if the first nine holes were pretty good, perhaps even great, making the turn is a time for intestinal fortitude and mental toughness to kick in as the golfer starts that final stretch.

There are some rich analogies that can be transferred to everyday life for the average individual. For instance, we all come to a point where we must make a decision about what kind of person we're going to be. Are we going to go our own way and trudge along in the rough, on the cart path, in the bunker or, at worst, in the hazards? Or are we going to take a stand, make that turn and start living a life that strives for integrity and, with God's help, stays in that proverbial fairway?

Making the turn might also represent an individual decision or a defining moment in life when, like that golfer looking to stay on a hot streak, it's time to finish strong and re-dedicate to that initial commitment of integrity. Regardless of which analogy fits best for any given person, sound moral character based on God's biblical standard is always a winning choice.

the turn

chapterTEN

"We were created not to sin. We were created to keep company with God in the Garden of Eden and have fellowship. All was supposed to be great. But we're the ones that messed that up. He created us with the ability to have integrity. He did not create us to mess up. That's evil pulling on us. Integrity matters to Him because we're His creation. We're His prized possession that He created in His image. When you're talking about something being in God's image, the person who has the most integrity would be God. He's consistent and true to His Word and we're created in His image. That's why it's important to God."

-- Adam Wainwright

Integrity Matters

"Who are we as men if no one can believe what we say?"[1]

Adam Wainwright brings up an interesting question that is all too relevant in this day and age. Trust between the general public and society's vaunted institutions is at an all-time low. Frequent integrity breaches amongst politicians, executives, entertainers, and even ministers have fractured the faith we once had in our leaders and created an unhealthy culture of cynicism.

"It feels like integrity matters less and less," Stewart Cink says. "It really does if you look at the big picture." But if you read the Bible, you'll find that integrity still matters whether it's, as Cink adds, "1900, 2011, or the year 3000."[2]

Cink's assertion is backed up by numerous passages found within the pages of God's Word. In his letter to the church of Philippi, the Apostle Paul explains the importance of righteous living. "Do everything without complaining or arguing," he writes, "so that you may become blameless and pure, children of God without fault in a crooked and depraved generation, in which you shine like stars in the universe as you hold out the word of life — in order that I may boast on the day of Christ that I did not run or labor for nothing" (Philippians 2:14–16).

Perhaps more than ever, Paul's words ring true in a world where we are judged, not for our hearts, but for our works.

"That's why it's important to have a good witness," Jonathan Byrd says. "We're God's ambassadors. My son is going to look at my life. My wife is going to look at my life. Other people are going to look at me from a larger platform than the average guy because I'm on TV and I'm in front of people. They'll look at me to see if there are any gaps or blind spots. If I'm saying one thing but doing something different, that's hypocritical. I don't profess to be perfect, but I want what I say to match up with how I walk and how I live my life. Otherwise, people won't take what I say very seriously. They're not going to take God and my faith seriously if I'm not a good ambassador for Him."[3]

Byrd's example, along with the example set by fellow veteran golfers such as Stewart Cink and Ben Crane, doesn't go unnoticed by some of the sports' rising stars. Rickie Fowler says he also feels the responsibility of being a role model and wants to live his life accordingly. "Playing good golf definitely draws attention, so I want to have a good attitude on the course and do the right things," Fowler says. "I'm definitely conscious that I'm being watched at all times. I don't want to be a screw-up or anything like that. I want to do the right things and set the right example."[4]

But beyond just being a positive role model or having a good witness, integrity matters because it allows us to give others a glimpse of God's character as we exemplify the character of Christ. In Matthew 5:14, Jesus calls us "the light of the world" and in Matthew 5:16, He challenges us to "let your light shine before (others), that they may see your good deeds and praise your Father in heaven."

"God desires us to live with integrity so we can be a light for Him — so we can be a light in a dark world," Ben Crane says. "When people live with integrity, they absolutely stand out."[5]

"It's what I try to remind myself of every day," PGA golfer Mark Wilson adds. "I'm always

trying to keep God's agenda in mind. Some days it's easier to do that than others, but even when we fall and fail in this game, we have to remember that people are watching. How we carry ourselves in the tough times might be the reason why someone wonders what's going on in our lives. It might make them want to investigate it. Hopefully, they'll see that the peace comes from Jesus. That's why I'm playing golf. That's why God gave me the talent. That's why I'm out here."[6]

Certainly professional athletes have a much larger platform than those of us in the general public, but that doesn't exempt us from shining that light to those around us. And when we live with godly integrity, our influence over others within our communities, work places and families will grow. In Proverbs 3:3–4, King Solomon advises us to "Let love and faithfulness never leave you; bind them around your neck, write them on the tablet of your heart. Then you will win favor and a good name in the sight of God and man."

"Integrity can completely build up your influence and your reputation," Wainwright says. "People seem to gravitate toward people who are doing things right and tend to run from people who aren't. If you're going to be the guy who people come to with their problems, then they have to know that they can trust you and that you're living that good, consistent lifestyle of integrity."[7]

The Perfect Life

Unfortunately, because of the decaying morality of today's world, it's getting more difficult to even know what true integrity looks like. But that's okay. We can always go straight to the source to find out exactly what encompasses godly righteousness — and not just by taking someone's word for it but by examining the earthly existence of Jesus Christ, the only one who has ever lived the perfect life.

"Being a Christian is more than saying, 'I believe' and then going about your merry way," Cink says. "God wants us to mimic Christ. One of the reasons He sent Christ was to give us an example of how to live. Think of what the world would be like if everyone tried to be Christ-like. There'd be no wars. There'd be no fighting. It would be a peaceful and happy world without these problems that we have. God wants us to be like Christ."[8]

Cink's sentiment echoes that of Paul who in 1 Corinthians 11:1 told the church members of Corinth to, "Follow my example, as I follow the example of Christ." But in order to do so, we must first understand His character. Of course, volumes of books could be written about the various nuances of this topic, so here are a few key points to consider when studying integrity as exemplified by God's Son:

1. Jesus was selfless

Even though He had every right not to be, Jesus was the perfect example of humility and selflessness. Consider this. When God warred against Lucifer and his minions, Jesus was there. When God created the heavens and the earth, Jesus was there. When God parted the Red Sea, Jesus was there. When God brought down the walls

of Jericho, Jesus was there. When God rescued Daniel from the lions, Jesus was there.

Jesus was at the right hand of the Father from the beginning and was there up until the moment He was sent to earth to take the form of a man. And since His departure over two thousand years ago, Jesus has rightly reclaimed His place in heaven.

Still, Paul writes in Philippians 2:6–8 that He, "being in very nature God, did not consider equality with God something to be grasped, but made himself nothing, taking the very nature of a servant, being made in human likeness. And being found in appearance as a man, he humbled himself and became obedient to death — even death on a cross!"

Paul's exclamation at the end of that passage serves as an indicator of just how much Jesus gave up to come to earth, live a nondescript life with no privilege, serve the interest of others, and ultimately give His life as a replacement for the debt mankind owed for its sin. Jesus' first act of integrity was displayed through His inconceivable selflessness, and we are likewise called to a life of humility.

"Do nothing out of selfish ambition or vain conceit, but in humility consider others better than yourselves. Each of you should look not only to your own interests but also to the interests of others" (Philippians 2:3–4).

2. Jesus was compassionate

So much of what Jesus did during His time on earth was driven by a supernatural love and compassion for people. The Gospels share many stories about how He was so easily moved at the sight of those who were hungry, hurting, sick, dying, and spiritually lost. Compassion is the extension of selflessness and humility. It takes us out of our comfort zone and forces us to act when we see others suffer from poverty, injustice, or just the effects of everyday life in a sinful world.

"Christ literally said that chief among his character traits was love," Cink says. "Along with that is respect. I feel like the life of integrity is embodied by love and respect for others. If you're a follower of Christ and an ambassador for Christ, you have no choice but to love and respect others."[9]

Jesus Himself bears this out with His famous response to the religious leaders looking to trap Him with the question, "What is the greatest commandment?"

"Love the Lord your God with all your heart and with all your soul and with all your mind and with all your strength. The second is this: Love your neighbor as yourself. There is no commandment greater than these" (Mark 12:30–31).

3. Jesus was just

When Cink talks about how the life of integrity is marked by love and respect for others, that's not just a reference to compassion but also to justice and fairness. And again, Jesus is the best example of what it looks like to treat all people — regardless of gender, race, religious affiliation, or social status — the same. There are many stories that chronicle this truth. He engaged the greedy tax collector Zacchaeus in conversation and spent time in his home (Luke 19:1–10). Jesus shared His Gospel message with the adulteress woman at the well (John 4:1–38) and shortly thereafter healed a royal official's child (John 4:43–54). He was also known to serve the needs of children, widows, lepers, religious leaders, outcasts, and the poor.

But divine justice is also evident in the way Jesus sees man's sinful nature. One of the most beautiful passages in the Bible is found in Romans 3:22–24. It contains a harsh reality accompanied by an unfathomable solution: "This righteousness from God comes through faith in Jesus Christ to all who believe. There is no difference, for all have sinned and fall short of the glory of God, and are justified freely by his grace through the redemption that came by Christ Jesus."

Not only is that incredible news for every single human being on the planet, divine justice as displayed through the life of Christ and through God's character also sets the standard for earthly integrity as it pertains to our relationships with others. We are called to show grace and forgiveness to those who hurt us and commanded to serve those around us who are in need, regardless of our differences.

4. Jesus was truthful

Ask a random person on the street to define the word "integrity" and it's likely that the majority will at some point invoke some reference to honesty or keeping one's word. Throughout the ages, telling the truth has been considered a key element of moral character and ethical behavior. But Jesus set the ultimate standard for integrity. He wasn't just 100 percent truthful — He was 100 percent truth!

"He is who He said He was," Wainwright concurs. "He said He was God's Son and everyone laughed at Him. He had some followers and those numbers grew, but at the end of the day, He was thrown up on a Cross and killed because of who He said He was. Three days later He rose again because He was who He said He was."[10]

Scripture backs up Christ's controversial claim. In Matthew 20:17–19, He foretold of his death and Resurrection. Not long after that, Jesus was unfairly tried, relentlessly mocked, brutally tortured, and crucified to His death on a Cross (Matthew 27:11–66). The second part of Jesus' prediction came true three days later when the tombstone that had been placed in front of his grave was removed by angels and a resurrected Savior emerged (Matthew 28:1–10).

Because of those world-changing events, Jesus proved another of His bold statements to be true. In John 14:6, He proclaimed: "I am the way and the truth and the life. No one comes to the Father except through me." Jesus is obviously the only one who can make that claim, but the mere fact that He embodies perfect truth serves as the impetus for us as His followers to embrace a life that is marked by honest, ethical conduct that reflects the truth that is living inside us.

5. Jesus was disciplined

Look at any person known for his or her integrity and chances are you'll find that he or she also employs a healthy dose of self-discipline. In Hebrews 12:11 it says that "all discipline seems painful rather than pleasant, but later it yields the peaceful fruit of righteousness to those have been trained by it" (ESV).

Jesus demonstrated what a disciplined life should look like. In Luke 4:14–16, we read that He customarily went to the synagogue to study the Scriptures from his childhood all the way into His adult years. Jesus understood the truth written by His ancestor David hundreds of years earlier: "I have hidden your word in my heart that I might not sin against you" (Psalm 119:11).

Jesus also took time every day to talk with the Father. As Luke noted in his Gospel account, He "often withdrew to lonely places and prayed" (Luke 5:16). Again, He had the foresight and godly wisdom that gave Him a keen understanding of how consistent communication with God would bring strength for the difficult journey ahead.

In Matthew 4:1–11, we find the story of Jesus' first major test. He was "led by the Spirit into the desert to be tempted by the devil" (verse 1) where He fasted 40 days and 40 nights. Satan tried on three separate occasions to get Jesus to sin, but every time, He quoted Scripture and maintained His integrity.

"Jesus wasn't persuaded by anyone or tempted by anyone, Satan included," D.J. Brigman says. "That's amazing to me because I know about my daily struggles to resist temptation and being influenced by other people. His mind was set right. He knew the right thing to do in every situation. When I'm faced with situations and I don't know what to do, I've learned to ask myself, What would Christ do in this situation? How would He handle it? Most of the time, it's the opposite of what my human nature would want me to do."[11]

Despite the fact that Jesus was fully man and fully God, He still made time for spiritual disciplines such as Bible devotion, prayer, and fasting. If Jesus felt the need for that level of commitment, how much more should we, as mere mortals, dedicate ourselves to those life-giving tools in order to cultivate the "fruit of righteousness"?

Making the Turn

For the follower of Christ, trying to live with His level of integrity might seem like the equivalent of a golfer with a 25 handicap trying to play as good as Tiger Woods or Phil Mickelson. But as discussed in the first chapter of this book, Jesus told His disciples to, "Be perfect, therefore, as your heavenly Father is perfect" (Matthew 5:48).

So what does that mean? How is it possible for imperfect people living in an imperfect world to be perfect as God is perfect? Here's a little secret for you. It's not. Jesus was sinless and we were born with sin in our hearts. So we started out already with a severe deficit in the quest for a perfect life.

But there's some good news to be found in 2 Corinthians 5:21: "God made (Jesus) who had no sin to be sin for us, so that in him we might become the righteousness of God."

That means this business about being perfect isn't about earning our salvation. We could never do enough to repay God for the sacrifice He made when He sent His Son to die for our sins. But rather, His desire for us to strive for perfection is all about some of those things mentioned earlier such as maintaining a good witness, gaining influence with non-believers, and being above reproach when we are attacked for our faith.

However, the biggest reason we should desire to strive for Christ-like integrity is so we can "purify ourselves from everything that contaminates body and spirit, perfecting holiness out of reverence for God" (2 Corinthians 7:1). In other words, we should have such a deep appreciation for our salvation and such a passionate love for God that we will offer our bodies "as living sacrifices, holy and pleasing to God" (Romans 12:1).

We will surely make mistakes and we no doubt have those moments when we sin against God and need to repent, but we don't have to let our humanness stop us from striving for integrity with His supernatural assistance. Here are a few things to consider while pursuing *Life in the Fairway*:

1. Follow Jesus

Before we can pursue godly integrity, we must first make the decision to accept Jesus as our Savior by confessing our sins and inviting Him to live inside our hearts (Romans 10:9). Once we make that life-changing choice, we must then accept the challenge to actively pursue a relationship with Him. In Luke 9:23, Jesus tells us that, "If anyone would come after me, he must deny himself and take up his cross daily and follow me."

And from there, as we continue to put self at the bottom of our priority list and keep Him at the top, we will experience a transformation that will allow us to be selfless, compassionate, just, truthful, and disciplined. Second Peter 1:3–4 shares this encouraging promise: "His divine power has given us everything we need for life and godliness through our knowledge of him who called us by his own glory and goodness. Through these he has given us his very great and precious promises, so that through them you may participate in the divine nature and escape the corruption in the world caused by evil desires."

2. Submit to the Spirit

Once we've made that decision to follow Christ and we've begun to study His character as a blueprint for our own walk toward integrity, there's no more important step than to actively pursue the guidance of the Spirit. When Jesus left the earth, He knew His followers couldn't face the challenges that lie ahead without some divine help. That's why in John 14:26, He promised them that "the Counselor, the Holy Spirit, whom the Father will send in my name, will teach you all things and remind you of everything I have said to you."

After the Holy Spirit arrived on the Day of Pentecost (chronicled in Acts 2), Jesus' followers were empowered to evangelize the world and strengthened to face the persecution that was coming their way. We also have access to that Holy Spirit and it's accompanying attributes. In fact, in Galatians 5:22–23 we find a list of characteristics that should be operating in our lives if we are allowing the Spirit to lead us: "But the fruit of the Spirit is love, joy, peace, longsuffering, kindness, goodness, faithfulness, gentleness, self-control. Against such there is no law" (NKJV).

A sure-fire way to know if we are walking in the Spirit is to honestly evaluate our lives and see if those fruits are actively present and helping us in our quest to consistently live with godly integrity.

3. Commit to spiritual discipline

Did Jesus really need to study the Scriptures? After all, He was the living, breathing Word of God. And did He really need to spend time in prayer? Jesus knew God's heart intimately. What more could He gain through that daily communication?

Perhaps it was because Jesus was equally man during His time on earth and He needed the strength to accomplish the task for which He had been sent. But there is something else. Jesus practiced spiritual disciplines as an example for His followers. He wanted us to see that prayer and Bible devotion were necessary for survival and the key to a successful Christian walk.

In 2 Timothy 3:16–17, Paul writes, "All Scripture is God-breathed and is useful for teaching, rebuking, correcting and training in righteousness, so that the (servant) of God may be thoroughly equipped for every good work."

"Almost every situation you find yourself in is dealt with directly in the Bible," Cink says. "God provided us this set of blueprints; this example in His Son for us to imitate and to mimic so that we know how to act when find ourselves in these situations. If we find ourselves in a hazard in life or you hit that proverbial shot out of bounds, and we all do sometimes, you've got to know where to go from there."[12]

And of course, that also requires an active prayer life in which we engage the Father in two-way conversation. It's not just about telling Him what we need or even thanking Him and praising Him, but it's also about taking time to listen for His voice and allowing His Spirit to work in our hearts.

In Hebrews 4:16, the writer says, "Let us then with confidence draw near to the throne of grace, that we may receive mercy and find grace to help in time of need" (ESV).

4. Set up an accountability system

While Christ's example, the guidance of the Holy Spirit, and the implementation of spiritual discipline are all powerful tools in this journey of integrity, the Bible also suggests another key to maintaining our character. Time and again, we read about the importance of Christian fellowship in the context of the Church, the Body of Christ, and even just amongst friends and family members who are like-minded in their beliefs.

This practice has become known as accountability, but it has been around for thousands of years. Solomon wrote often on the subjects. He tells us in Proverbs 27:17 that, "As iron sharpens iron, so one (person) sharpens another."

"The guys that hold me accountable and mentor me are the kind of guys that aren't afraid to ask me tough questions," Webb Simpson says. "One of the first things one of my mentors asked me when I hadn't talked to him in a while was, 'How is your wife? How is your marriage?' It is so important, especially among men, to share with each other and not hold anything back and be able to be vulnerable. I've seen so many men that are trying so hard to be the tough man and they won't let anybody in. They're hiding all these things, these secrets. It's so freeing to be able to get things out. That's one thing that my mentors have helped me with. So much fruit can come from confession and repentance."[13]

There's also a certain strength that comes in numbers. As Ecclesiastes 4:12 says, "Though one may be overpowered, two can defend themselves."

Perhaps that explains why Jonathan Byrd admittedly struggles when he doesn't have accountability in his life. "There's a period of time when I feel like I'm doing okay, but I just drift," he adds. "My life just drifts away from the path that I'm supposed to be on. I've got some awesome godly men in my life that keep me accountable and ask me the tough questions. When I don't have that in my life, I get stale in my walk with God."[14]

5. Take courage

Finally, living with godly integrity requires a certain measure of courage. First of all, it takes courage to do the right things no matter the consequences or no matter how dire the situation might seem. In the Old Testament, there are numerous stories about courageous men and women that followed God regardless of what peril awaited them. Noah, Job, Joseph, and Daniel are just a few of the iconic Bible heroes who walked with integrity under the most extreme circumstances — sometimes even staring down possible death in the process.

Joseph was another courageous man of integrity. After Moses died, God appointed him to lead the Children of Israel across the Jordan River and into a land that was occupied by powerful armies and unknown dangers. The Lord gave a powerful charge to embolden the young leader. "Be strong and very courageous. Be careful to obey all the law my servant Moses gave you; do not turn from it to the right or to the left, that you may be successful wherever you go. Do not let this Book of the Law depart from your mouth; meditate on it day and night, so that you may be careful to do everything written in it. Then you will be prosperous and successful. Have I not commanded you? Be strong and courageous. Do not be terrified; do not be discouraged, for the Lord your God will be with you wherever you go" (Joshua 1:7–9).

"God doesn't recommend we banish fear from our lives," Kevin Streelman says. "He commands it. That really pushes me daily. What He did with Joshua at that time is inspiring. He was scared to cross the river but God said, 'It's time to go. I'm telling you to do this.' So many times in this life, we want to follow our own path instead of listening to what the Lord wants us to do, but He promises us so much more fulfillment when we let Him take over."[15]

It also takes courage to admit and correct mistakes, and then to move forward instead of getting mired in guilt or worse, taking steps backward and regressing into those old, sinful ways. David is one of the Bible's best examples of this principle. His sins are well documented, yet the Book of Acts tells us that God "testified concerning him: 'I have found David son of Jesse a man after my own heart; he will do everything I want him to do' " (Acts 13:22).

"You just have to admit it and be honest with yourself, with God and with others and say, 'Hey, I made a mistake," Cink advises. "Ask for forgiveness, do everything you can to not make that mistake again and make it up to anyone you've hurt."[16]

And once we've taken that step, we can follow Paul's advice who writes, "Forgetting what is behind and straining toward what is ahead, I press on toward the goal to win the prize for which God has called me heavenward in Christ Jesus" (Philippians 3:13–14).

Integrity Has No End

To once again be clear, integrity is not the path to salvation. Romans 3:20 reminds us that "no one will be declared righteous in (God's) sight by observing the law; rather, through the law we become conscious of sin."

Integrity, on the other hand, is the outward expression of what God has done in our hearts and the evidence that the Holy Spirit is guiding and directing our steps. Integrity also allows us to do

those things mentioned earlier in this chapter. It gives us influence. It preserves our witness. And as many of the golfers in this book have discussed, it brings peace, freedom, and abundant life.

Integrity also protects us from the harsh consequences of sinful behavior. And that's why it's important to remember that integrity has no end. One bad decision can have serious consequences. Straying from integrity even for a moment can fatally wound a relationship. It can snatch away a life-altering opportunity. It can limit one's personal freedom. And immoral choices, even in the slightest form, can inflict physical damage on others and us — quite possibly even death.

That's why integrity doesn't take a day off. It isn't compartmentalized. We can't have integrity in one area of our life but not another. That lack of moral clarity will catch up to us eventually, although it might seem as if we're "getting away with it" for a time.

And because integrity often causes us to choose between what our flesh wants and what is actually best for us, the decision to live the righteous life is simply all about pride versus selflessness. Wainwright says he spent a couple of years searching for the perfect Scripture to challenge him to strive for Christ-like integrity. He finally landed on Acts 20:24 where Paul's words to the early church elders still resonate today: "I consider my life worth nothing to me, if only I may finish the race and complete the task the Lord Jesus has given me — the task of testifying to the gospel of God's grace."

"As Christians, the number one thing we're called to do is to spread the Word of God," Wainwright says. "You cannot do that without living the life of integrity."[17]

It's a choice to live with integrity. And it's not an easy choice. In Matthew 7:13–14, Jesus confirms that truth when He commands us to, "Enter through the narrow gate. For wide is the gate and broad is the road that leads to destruction, and many enter through it. But small is the gate and narrow the road that leads to life, and only a few find it."

"Integrity is the best way," Byrd simply concludes. "God said that He is the source of all that is good. He'll give us life to the fullest if we follow Him. If we do that, it's just the best way. It's a narrow path. It's the more difficult path than the wide road, but it's the best way."[18]

Charitable Organizations & Ministries

The following is a list of charitable organizations and ministries with which the athletes featured in this book are involved:

Catch-A-Dream Foundation
(662) 325-8149
www.catchadream.org

College Golf Fellowship
www.collegegolffellowship.com

Golden Isles FCA
(912) 279-0807
www.goldenislesfca.org

FCA Golf/Tour Life
(904) 273-9541
golfinfo@fca.org
www.fcagolf.org

The Healing Place
(256) 383-7133
www.thehealingplaceinfo.org

Hope Farm
(817) 926-9116
hopefarm@hopefarminc.org
www.hopefarminc.org

Love 146
(203) 772-4420
info@love146.org
www.love146.org

Search Ministries
(800) 61-SEARCH
www.searchnational.org

St. Bernard Project
(504) 277-6831
www.stbernardproject.org

Young Life
(877) 438-9572
www.younglife.org/us

"One of the greatest teachings in the Bible is the contrast between Christ's life and the disciples. The biggest example I always think of is the woman at the well. They go into town. He stays at the well. The woman comes out to the well. She's got a bad reputation. She's had four or five husbands. The man she's living with isn't even her husband. She was a scourge of the town in everyone's mind. What does Jesus do? He offers her living water and everlasting life. He talks to her and he cares for her. He serves her. This wretch of the town, He serves her. When everybody comes out to see Christ, they're all amazed and dismayed that He's even speaking to her. He puts them in their place quickly and says, 'This is the right thing to do.' The contrast between how He acted and how His disciples acted is vivid and tells us a lot about the way we should be in the world."

— Stewart Cink

When Roberto De Vicenzo teed off for the final round of the 1968 Masters, he had no idea that a rules change from 21 years earlier would play such a vital role later that day. De Vicenzo thought he had forced a play-off with Bob Goalby. But unfortunately, he had signed an incorrect scorecard. On the 17th hole, De Vicenzo made a score of 3, good for a birdie, but his playing partner Tommy Aaron, who was keeping De Vicenzo's scorecard, put down a 4 instead. Even though De Vicenzo shot a 65 that day, he was instead credited with a 66. His shot at the Masters was gone.

"What a stupid I am to be wrong here," De Vicenzo told reporters after the incident.[1]

According to USGA Museum curator and historian Michael Trostel, "The USGA authored the Rules of Golf in 1947. Rule 20(6) [formerly Rule 5] now required that 'on competition of the stipulated round the card shall be signed by the marker and the competitor, who shall see that it is handed in as soon as possible.' Thus, we have the first instance in the Rules where the competitor was responsible for signing the card in addition to his marker."[2]

This rule "provides accountability" as the golfer is "validating his score to the rest of the field as accurate," Trostel adds. "As such, when the player signs and validates his scorecard, he influences the judgments of all others in the field. This influence cannot be undone — hence the penalty of disqualification for signing an incorrect scoreboard."[3]

For instance, if a player knows he needs to shoot a birdie on the 18th hole in order to force a play-off with another player that has already completed his round, he will shoot in such a manner as to give himself the best opportunity to make the required score.

Initially, this rule might seem to be about providing an environment of accountability amongst the players. But it also requires each golfer to take responsibility for his or her actions even if, as in the case of De Vicenzo, the mistake unintentionally gives an opponent the advantage.

And while this cautionary tale might speak to the issues of accountability and integrity, there's actually something else that catches Kevin Streelman's attention. "All it takes is one screwup and one's name can be tainted within the golfing world for many years to come," he adroitly notes.[4]

De Vicenzo's name wasn't tainted due to suspicion of cheating. Who would actually add a stroke to their scorecard on purpose? But he is now forever known for making one of the most costly mistakes in PGA Tour history. Streelman's point still applies. It truly does just take one mistake to change the direction of someone's life. This is especially true for those who willfully go against godly integrity.

That's why the Apostle Paul reminds us in 1 Timothy 1:18–19 to "fight the good fight, keeping faith a good conscience, which some have rejected and suffered shipwreck in regard to their faith" (NAS).

Endnotes

Chapter 1

[1] Aaron Baddeley, interview with the author, April 3, 2006.

[2] Ibid.

[3] D.J. Brigman, interview with the author, August 9, 2011.

[4] Ben Crane, interview with the author, August 4, 2011.

[5] Stewart Cink, interview with the author, July 27, 2011.

[6] Ibid.

[7] Ben Crane, interview with the author, August 4, 2011.

[8] Ibid.

[9] Aaron Baddeley, interview with the author, July 16, 2011.

[10] Aaron Baddeley, interview with the author, October 29, 2011.

[11] D.J. Brigman, interview with the author, August 9, 2011.

[12] Ibid.

[13] Ibid.

[14] Ibid.

[15] Ibid.

[16] Ben Crane, interview with the author, August 4, 2011.

[17] D.J. Brigman, interview with the author, August 9, 2011.

[18] Stewart Cink, interview with the author, July 27, 2011.

[19] D.J. Brigman, interview with the author, August 9, 2011.

[20] Ibid.

Chapter 2

[1] Jonathan Byrd, interview with the author, October 11, 2011.

[2] Ibid.

[3] Ibid.

[4] Ibid.

[5] Ibid.

[6] ESPN.com, 2011 PGA Tour Money List, http://espn.go.com/golf/moneylist/_/page/5/year/2011 (accessed Feb. 24, 2012).

[7] Dennis Cauchon and Barbara Hansen, "Typical U.S. Family Got Poorer During the Past 10 Years," USAToday.com, http://www.usatoday.com/news/nation/story/2011-09-13/census-household-income/50383882/1 (September 14, 2011).

[8] Jonathan Byrd, interview with the author, October 11, 2011.

[9] Ibid.

[10] Ibid.

[11] Ibid.

[12] Ibid.

[13] Ibid.

[14] Ibid.

[15] Ibid.

[16] Ibid.

[17] The United States Golf Association and R&A Rules Limited, USGA Rules of Golf, 2012.

[18] Jonathan Byrd, interview with the author, October 11, 2011.

[19] Ibid.

[20] Ibid.

[21] Ibid.

[22] Jonathan Byrd, interview with the author, December 12, 2011.

[23] PGA Tour, Jonathan Byrd profile, http://www.pgatour.com/golfers/024925/jonathan-byrd (accessed February 24, 2012).

Chapter 3

1 Nick Poppa, "Golf's Inception," http://www.jimmillergolf.com/golfsinception.html (accessed February 21, 2012).

2 Gary Wiren, interview with the author, May 23, 2011.

3 Ibid.

4 Rand Jerris, interview with the author, May 20, 2011.

5 Rand Jerris, interview with the author, February 23, 2012.

6 Rand Jerris, interview with the author, May 20, 2011.

7 Ibid.

Chapter 4

[1] PGA Tour, Webb Simpson profile, http://www.pgatour.com/golfers/029221/webb-simpson (accessed January 6, 2012).

[2] NOAA Satellite and Information Service, Average Wind Speed, http://www.ncdc.noaa.gov/oa/climate/online/ccd/avgwind.html (accessed January 7, 2012).

[3] Brian Wacker, "Penalty Costs Simpson Again," http://tourreport.pgatour.com/2011/05/01/penalty-costs-simpson-again (May 1, 2011).

[4] Ibid.

[5] Webb Simpson, interview with the author, October 11, 2011.

[6] Ibid.

[7] PGA Tour Leaderboard, 2011 Zurich Classic of New Orleans, http://sports.yahoo.com/golf/pga/leaderboard/2011/12 (accessed January 7, 2012).

[8] PGA Tour, Statistics, http://www.pgatour.com/r/stats (accessed January 6, 2012).

[9] Webb Simpson, interview with the author, October 11, 2011.

[10] Ibid.

[11] Tom Lehman, response to question by the author during press conference at the Crowne Plaza Invitational at the Colonial in Fort Worth, Texas, May 17, 2011.

[12] Webb Simpson, interview with the author, October 11, 2011.

[13] D.J. Brigman, interview with the author, August 9, 2011.

[14] Ibid.

[15] Webb Simpson, interview with the author, October 11, 2011.

[16] Ibid.

[17] Wake Forest Sports, Webb Simpson profile, http://www.wakeforestsports.com/sports/m-golf/mtt/simpson_webb00.html (accessed January 10, 2012).

[18] Sun Bowl Golf, Past Winners, http://sunbowlgolf.org/#/#/history/2 (accessed January 10, 2012).

[19] Webb Simpson, interview with the author, October 11, 2011.

[20] Ibid.

[21] Ibid.

[22] Caddy Bytes, http://www.caddybytes.com/Peter_Coleman_and_Langer.htm (accessed January 11, 2012).

[23] Jim McCabe, "Caddie's illness inspiring Simpson on Tour," http://www.golfweek.com/news/2010/jun/29/caddies-illness-inspiring-simpson-tour (June 29, 2010).

[24] Ibid.

[25] Webb Simpson, interview with the author, October 11, 2011.

[26] Ron Green Jr., "Simpson, Caddie a Strong Mix," http://www.newsobserver.com/2011/08/25/1434329/simpson-caddie-a-strong-mix.html, (August 21, 2011).

[27] [27] Webb Simpson, interview with the author, October 11, 2011.

[28] Ibid.

[29] Ibid.

[30] Ibid.

[31] Ibid.

[32] Ibid.

[33] Dictionary.com, "Integrity," http://dictionary.reference.com/browse/integrity (accessed January 12, 2012).

[34] Webb Simpson, interview with the author, October 11, 2011.

[35] Ibid.

[36] Ibid.

[37] Ibid.

[38] Ibid.

[39] Ibid.

[40] Ibid.

[41] PGA.com Wire Services Series, "Golfers 'Given a Break' by Updates to Multiple Rules by USGA and R&A," http://www.pga.com/news/industry-news/usga-ra-announce-new-rules-golf-2012 (accessed January 9, 2012).

[42] Webb Simpson, interview with the author, October 11, 2011.

[43] Ibid.

[44] PGA Tour, Webb Simpson profile, http://www.pgatour.com/golfers/029221/webb-simpson (accessed January 6, 2012)

Chapter 5

[1] Bernhard Langer, interview with the author, Oct. 10, 2011.

[2] CBS Sports, The Players Championship Leaderboard, http://www.cbssports.com/golf/leaderboard/pga-tour/450085/the-players-championship (May 15, 2011).

[3] ESPN.com, Reno-Tahoe Open Leaderboard, http://espn.go.com/golf/leaderboard?tournamentId=920 (August 7, 2011).

[4] Kevin Streelman, interview with the author, May 24, 2011.

[5] Ibid.

[6] Jonathan Byrd, interview with the author, October 11, 2011.

[7] Stewart Cink, interview with the author, July 27, 2011.

[8] Webb Simpson, interview with the author, October 11, 2011.

Chapter 6

[1] Stewart Cink, interview with the author, July 27, 2011.

[2] Ibid.

[3] PGA Tour, Stewart Cink profile, http:// http://www.pgatour.com/golfers/020229/stewart-cink (accessed January 29, 2012).

[4] Stewart Cink, interview with the author, July 27, 2011.

[5] Ibid.

[6] Ibid.

[7] Ibid.

[8] Ibid.

[9] Ibid.

[10] Jonathan Byrd, interview with the author, October 11, 2011.

[11] Morris Pickens, interview with the author, June 8, 2011.

[12] Stewart Cink, interview with the author, July 27, 2011.

13 Ibid.

14 Ibid.

15 Ibid.

16 Ibid.

17 Ibid.

18 Ibid.

19 Brent Kelley, "Waste Area," golf.about.com/od/golfterms/g/waste-area.htm (accessed January 29, 2012).

20 Stewart Cink, interview with the author, July 27, 2011.

21 Ibid.

22 Ibid.

23 Ibid.

24 Ibid.

25 Ibid.

26 Ibid.

27 Ibid.

28 Ibid.

29 PGA Tour, Stewart Cink profile, http:// http://www.pgatour.com/golfers/020229/stewart-cink (accessed January 29, 2012).

Chapter 7

1 D.J. Brigman, interview with the author, August 9, 2011.

2 Rand Jerris, interview with the author, May 20, 2011.

3 Ibid.

4 Gary Wiren, interview with the author, May 23, 2011.

5 Ibid.

6 Rand Jerris, interview with the author, May 20, 2011.

7 GaryWiren.com, Gary Wiren biography, http://www.garywiren.com/index.php?gw=biography (accessed February 4, 2012).

8 Gary Wiren, interview with the author, May 23, 2011.

9 Jonathan Byrd, interview with the author, October 11, 2011.

Chapter 8

1 Ben Crane, interview with the author, August 4, 2011.

2 ESPN News Services, "Sabbatini apologizes to Crane after snapping," http://sports.espn.go.com/golf/news/story?id=2084472 (June 14, 2005).

3 Ibid.

4 Ben Crane, interview with the author, August 4, 2011.

5 Ibid.

6 Ibid.

7 Ibid.

8 Ibid.

9 Ibid.

10 Ibid.

11 Ibid.

12 Ibid.

13 Ibid.

14 Ibid.

15 Ibid.

16 Ibid.

17 Ibid.

18 Ibid.

19 Ibid.

20 PGA Tour, Ben Crane profile, http://www.pgatour.com/golfers/023541/ben-crane (accessed February 12, 2012).

Chapter 9

Justin Leonard endnotes

1 PGA Tour, Justin Leonard profile, http://www.pgatour.com/golfers/010860/justin-leonard (accessed Feb. 9, 2012).

2 Ibid.

3 Jeff Hopper, "Reward In Sight," http://www.linksplayers.com/Player_Profiles/Justin_Leonard/justin_leonard.html (accessed February 9, 2012).

4 Ibid.

5 Ibid.

6 Ibid.

Aaron Baddeley endnotes

1 USA Today, "Furyk, Baddeley tied for lead at Verizon Heritage," http://www.usatoday.com/sports/golf/pga/2006-04-15-verizon-heritage_x.htm, April 16, 2006.

2 Aaron Baddeley, interview with the author, April 3, 2006.

3 The-Sport.org, Verizon Heritage Final Results, http://www.the-sports.org/golf-verizon-heritage-hilton-head-open-2006-results-men-s7-c0-b0-g41-t1390-u51-m14363-v1.html, April 16, 2006.

4 Aaron Baddeley, interview with the author, April 3, 2006.

5 Aaron Baddeley, interview with the author, July 16, 2011.

6 Aaron Baddeley, interview with the author, April 3, 2006.

7 Chad Bonham, "Good To Be Badds," New Man, July/August 2006.

8 Aaron Baddeley, interview with the author, April 3, 2006.

9 Jonathan Byrd, interview with the author, December 12, 2011.

10 Bonham, "Good To Be Badds."

11 Aaron Baddeley, interview with the author, July 16, 2011.

12 Aaron Baddeley, interview with the author, October 29, 2011.

13 Aaron Baddeley, interview with the author, April 3, 2006.

14 PGA Tour, Aaron Baddeley profile, http://www.pgatour.com/golfers/022371/aaron-baddeley (accessed Feb. 2, 2012).

Kevin Streelman endnotes

1 Kevin Streelman, interview with the author, May 18, 2011.

2 Ibid.

3 Kevin Streelman, interview with the author, May 24, 2011.

4 Ibid.

5 Ibid.

6 Ibid.

7 Ibid.

8 PGA Tour, Kevin Streelman profile, http://www.pgatour.com/golfers/027214/kevin-streelman (accessed Jan. 31, 2012).

D.J. Brigman endnotes

1 D.J. Brigman, interview with the author, August 9, 2011.

2 Ibid.

3 Ibid.

4 PGA Tour, D.J. Brigman Profile, http://www.pgatour.com/golfers/024290/dj-brigman (accessed January 9, 2012).

5 D.J. Brigman, interview with the author, August 9, 2011.

6 Ibid.

7 Ibid.

8 Ibid.

9 Ibid.

10 PGA Tour, D.J. Brigman Profile, http://www.pgatour.com/golfers/024290/dj-brigman (accessed January 9, 2012).

Bernhard Langer endnotes

1 Bernhard Langer, interview with the author, October 10, 2011.

2 Bernhard Langer, interview with the author, March 16, 2004.

3 Chad Bonham, "The Masters Plan," New Man, July/August 2005.

4 Ibid.

5 Ibid.

6 Bernhard Langer, interview with the author, October 10, 2011.

7 PGA Tour, Bernhard Langer profile, http://www.pgatour.com/golfers/001666/bernhard-langer/ (accessed January 31, 2012).

8 Bernhard Langer, interview with the author, October 10, 2011.

9 PGA Tour, Bernhard Langer profile, http://www.pgatour.com/golfers/001666/bernhard-langer/ (accessed January 31, 2012).

Chapter 10

1 Adam Wainwright, interview with the author, May 11, 2011.

2 Stewart Cink, interview with the author, July 27, 2011.

3 Jonathan Byrd, interview with the author, Dec. 12, 2011.

4 Rickie Fowler, interview with the author, May 18, 2011.

5 Ben Crane, interview with the author, Aug. 4, 2011.

6 Mark Wilson, interview with the author, May 18, 2011.

7 Adam Wainwright, interview with the author, May 11, 2011.

8 Stewart Cink, interview with the author, July 27, 2011.

9 Ibid.

10 Adam Wainwright, interview with the author, May 11, 2011.

11 D.J. Brigman, interview with the author, Aug. 9, 2011.

12 Stewart Cink, interview with the author, July 27, 2011.

13 Webb Simpson, interview with the author, Oct.11, 2011.

14 Jonathan Byrd, interview with the author, Oct. 11, 2011.

15 Kevin Streelman, interview with the author, May 24, 2011.

16 Stewart Cink, interview with the author, July 27, 2011.

17 Adam Wainwright, interview with the author, May 11, 2011.

18 Jonathan Byrd, interview with the author, Dec.12, 2011.

Signing the Scorecard

1 Sobel, Jason, "Forty years later, De Vicenzo's gaffe remains unbelievable," http://sports.espn.go.com/golf/masters08/columns/story?columnist=sobel_jason&id=3324061, April 5, 2008.

2 Michael Trostel, interview with the author, February 6, 2012.

3 Ibid.

4 Kevin Streelman, interview with the author, May 24, 2011.

Along with *Life in the Fairway*, Chad Bonham has authored or co-authored twelve books including: *Wrestling with God*, *Spiritual Journeys*, Fellowship of Christian Athletes Core Value Series: *Excellence*, *Teamwork*, *Serving* and *Integrity*. He also writes for publications such as Charisma, Sharing the Victory, Ministries Today, Sports Spectrum, Beliefnet.com and many more. When he's not writing, Chad lends his efforts to various independent television and film projects. He was the coordinating producer for *Choosing Life (2010)* and *Life Happens (2011)*.

Chad and his wife Amy reside in Broken Arrow, Oklahoma with their three sons.

Let Chad know you are reading *Life in the Fairway* and learn about his upcoming projects by connecting with him online:

f facebook.com/**chadbonham**

t twitter.com/**chadbonham**

features.beliefnet.com/inspiringathletes

Enjoy a **FREE** download of *Life in the Fairway* discussion questions from each chapter at **nlpg.com/lifeinthefairway**

Hosting, Sponsoring, or Planning a Golf Tournament?

Reading *Life in the Fairway* can be a life-changing event for all who participate in the game.

Offer *Life in the Fairway* as a gift to the players.

Call **800.999.3777** for a generous discount on your order.

Tim Dudley

President & CEO
New Leaf Publishing Group